The Women's Press Ltd
34 Great Sutton Street, London EC1V 0DX

Amanda Hopkinson, biographer, journalist and campaigner, has travelled extensively in Central America, and is the translator of Claribel Alegría's *They Won't Take Me Alive* (The Women's Press, 1987).

Her biography of photographer Julia Margaret Cameron was published in 1986. She has four children and lives in London.

Amanda Hopkinson, editor

Lovers
and Comrades

Women's Resistance Poetry
from Central America

Translated by Amanda Hopkinson and
members of the El Salvador Solidarity
Campaign Cultural Committee

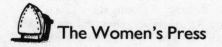 The Women's Press

First published by The Women's Press Limited 1989
A member of the Namara Group
34 Great Sutton Street, London EC1V 0DX

British Library Cataloguing in Publication Data

Lovers and comrades: women's resistance
   poetry from Central America.
   1. Poetry in Spanish. Central American
   women writers, 1945–. Anthologies
   I. Hopkinson, Amanda
   861

   ISBN 0-7043-4095-X

Typeset by M.C. Typeset Ltd
Printed and bound in Great Britain by
Cox & Wyman Reading Berks

Grateful acknowledgement is given for the following
sources:
Diana Avila, 'Concerning a Poetry Anthology', *El Sueño ha
Terminado* (San José, Costa Rica, 1976); Janina Fernández,
'Reflections', 'To Inactive Intellectuals', 'Certainty' and
'Costa Rica', *Certeza* (San José, 1982). Luz Méndez de la
Vega, 'Prologue', *Eva sin Dios* (Guatemala City, Guatemala,
1979); 'Fragile God', *De las Palabras y la Sombra* (Guatemala
City, 1984); 'The Heavenly Family', *Las Voces Silenciadas*
(Guatemala City, 1985). Vidaluz Meneses, 'Mother', *Llama
Guardada* (Managua, Nicaragua, 1975); 'Last Postcard to
my Father, General Meneses', 'In the New Country' and
'Minimum Homage' *El Aire que me Llama*, (Managua, 1982).
Claudia Lars, 'Poet', 'My Refuge', 'I Could Have Lived', 'A
Whole Lifetime', 'So You Never Reply', *Obras Escogidas* (San
Salvador, El Salvador, 1973); 'The New Woman Speaks'
and 'Yesterday's Child', *Poesía Femenina de El Salvador* (San

Salvador, 1975). Eulalia Bernard, 'Black Christ', 'A Happy Childhood', 'Requiem for my Jamaican Cousin', 'We are the Nation of Threes' and 'Metamorphosis of your Memory', *Ritmohéroe* (San José, 1982). Nancy Morejón, 'Black Woman' and 'Confession', *Collected Works* (Havana, Cuba, 1983). Rosario Murillo, 'In the Street, a Light', 'It Hurts' and 'Blanca, Like a Giant Lily', *En las Esplendidas Ciudades* (Managua, 1985). Gioconda Belli, 'The Blood of Others', 'Patria Libre: 19 July 1979', *Truenos y Arco Iris* (Managua, 1982); 'What Are You, Nicaragua?', 'Strike', (Línea de Fuego, 1978); 'And . . . ', 'Maternity', *Sobre la Grama* (1974), collected in *Amor Insurrecto* (Managua, 1984). Alaíde Foppa, 'Exile', 'Woman', 'Watermelon', *Poesía* (Guatemala City, 1982); 'Time' and 'Prayers', *Poetisas Desmitificadoras Guatemaltecas* (Guatemala City, 1984). Reina María Rodríguez, 'When a Woman Doesn't Sleep', 'The Awkward Line' and 'Today Fidel Speaks', *Cuando una Mujer no Duerme* (Havana, 1982). June Beer, 'Love Poem', *Nicaragua Today* (London, 1987). Ana María Rodas, 'Death of the Parents', 'Childhood Games', *Cuatro Esquinas del Juego de una Muñeca* (Guatemala City, 1975); 'Now I know', 'Mr Revolutionary', 'We Stopped at the Crossroads', *Poemas de la Izquierda Erótica* (Guatemala City, 1973). Maura Echevarría, 'From my Childhood', 'Phone Call from my Mother', *Ritual del Silencio* (San Salvador, 1984). Cony Pacheco, 'Just like María', *Poesía Libre 5* (Managua, 1982); Esmeralda Davila, 'To My Son' and 'In the Mountains', *Somos* (Managua, 1983–4). María Pineda, 'Orlando'; Julia Chavarría, 'The Letter'; Mirna Ojeda 'Salvador', *Talleres de Poesía – Antología* (Managua, 1983). Ana Istarú, 'A Crescent Moon', 'This Net Binds Me Tight', *La Estación de Fiebre* (San José, 1984). Soledad Cruz, 'Memorandum', 'Beginnings of Development', *Documentos de la Otra* (Havana, 1987). Claribel Alegría, 'I am a Mirror', 'Once We were Three', 'Confession' and 'Little Tamales from Cambray', *Sobrevivo* (Havana, 1978); 'Little Homeland', *Aprendizaje* (San Salvador, 1970); 'Everything is Normal in our Backyard', *Suma y Sigue* (Madrid, 1981). Michèle Najlis, 'The Dead', *Augurios* (San José, 1981); 'They Pursued Us Through the Night' and 'We the Children of the Sun', *Poesia Politica* (Managua, 1979). Lilly Guardia, 'I am Taut', 'I Sing, 'I Was About to Say' and 'A Child has Died', *Suenos de Canela* (San

José, 1986). Zaída Dormuz, 'The Final Offensive', *Talleres de Poesía de la Nueva Nicaragua* (Nicaragua, 1985). Daisy Zamora, 'Song of Hope', 'Tegucigalpa–Managua', 'To Comrade Blas Real Espinales', 'The Departure' and 'The Departure II', *La Violenta Espuma* (Managua, 1981). Marilyn Bobes, 'Love Story as Related by One of the Parties', *Bohemia* (Havana, 1983). Carmen Matute, 'Letter to a Lover', 'Island' and 'Your Name, Guatemala', *Poeta Solo* (Guatemala City, 1986). Corina Bruni, 'Valiant Homeland', *Altibajos* (San Salvador, 1984).

Contents

Bright Country

Woman in my Time

Lovers and Comrades

In the Struggle

Time of Awakening

Diana Avila *Costa Rica*

Concerning a Poetry Anthology

comrades
friends
enemies
the words
explosive
noisy
gentle
drops of honey in the ears
blows below the belt.
Let them struggle for love and smiles and hunger.

Introduction

Poetry is an important part of daily life in Latin America. It appears in newspapers and is recited on the radio, has a living oral as well as literary tradition, and has long been composed by women as well as men. A page of poetry published there may look little different from one here. But poetry in Latin America is meant to be heard as well as read. At parties and *peñas*, at social and political gatherings, at the most formal and the most domestic ceremonies related to the church and the family, poetry is a part of life; a number of significantly different cultural practices has blended in popular custom.

Over the last twenty years there has been a rapid acceleration in the quantity of Latin American texts translated into English. What was once praised as exotic (or patronised as folkloric) is now generally fashionable. Yet within this minor boom in literary imports, women's writing in general and their poetry in particular is still underrepresented. Of the forty-six poets included in this volume, barely half a dozen have had their work translated, and only half of these have had their collected works published. Yet, with the exception of the workshop and student writers, almost all are well known at home. Thus, for example, the works of the Chilean Pablo Neruda are widely available in a variety of English translations; but those of his no less eminent fellow national Gabriela Mistral, almost not at all. Roque Dalton, cast in the mould of the guerrilla-poet whose early and Byronic death has helped make him a much-sung national hero, is well published abroad, whereas Claribel Alegría, his prolific and acclaimed compatriot, has had to wait until her sixties to receive similar international recognition.

Yet women have traditionally written poetry in Latin America, much as they have written novels there. From the time of Sor Juana Inés de la Cruz (1651–95), the 'tenth muse' of colonial Mexico who composed extensive poetry in both Aztec and Spanish, through to the present day, women poets have been among the most outstanding writers in the region. And it is only now that many women writers are beginning to permit themselves the often longer stretches of time and concentration that allow for the construction of a full-length novel. It is no coincidence that Sor Juana, whose long songs and epics required such sustained dedication, was a nun, nor that the choice between family life and full-time writing is still a real one for many women.

Since the last century the poets seeking to combine the two have tended to divide themselves into two camps. There are the *poetisas* or 'lady poets' who produce interminably for newspapers, particularly in Guatemala and no self-respecting daily there would be without its poetry page. Patience Strong is probably our nearest equivalent, although few *poetisas* restrict themselves to her quatrains of moral homilies. Many column inches are expended in essentially bourgeois platitudes on the delights of spring and the cares of motherhood and in rhymes the equivalent of the moon-spoon-June variety. One committed feminist, the poet and former newspaper columnist Ana María Rodas, commented of the phenomenon in her native country: 'People write poetry all over the world. Guatemala's problem is that here it all gets published.' It was to break with this tradition that Ana María and a group of colleagues set up their own imprint, RIN – 78, ten years ago. The group functions as a mutual support and criticism forum as well as a publishing enterprise still prolific in producing the most radical new poetry in the country.

Their work falls within the second group, the *poetas*, whose poetry appears on xeroxed or even hand-written sheets and whose schedule of publications is at best erratic. Yet published or not, these poets' reputations rest on the actual achievement of their work and the women describe themselves as poets even when working full time at more purely administrative occupations. Curiously enough, *poeta* defies the norms of Spanish grammar in having a feminine ending regardless of which gender it is applied to. It is also acknowledged as an official term of address, and a letter can be designated to '*Poeta* X' in the same way as we might write Dr or Professor.

This suggests a level of status, if not of income, that is unusual here. It is, however, no easier to define a 'professional' poet in Central America than in England. Is it someone who has gained a recognisable academic qualification or undergone a relevant apprenticeship? In which case – as in so many other fields – there are women who have proved themselves repeatedly, obtaining university degrees and lectureships and studying under some of the region's finest poets. Or is a professional someone who works an accredited number of hours and earns a regular income by their industry? The first supposition defies the classical preferences for 'ivory tower' poetry and would eliminate some of the most famous names of western literature. The second is simply unrealistic, even given print-runs phenomenal by European standards. For even in Cuba and Nicaragua where, US-imposed economic blockades permitting, 15–20,000 copies may be printed at a single run, authors actually earn almost nothing by way of either advance or royalties. And even an economically stable country like Costa Rica, with no shortage of newsprint or paper to worry about, starves the most enterprising of its publishing houses (EDUCA, at the Central American university) and offers the pittance of $50 prizes and the kudos of being published by way of payment to its writers.

Most writers included here cannot work more than part time at best. Some salvage the mornings for their poetry before continuing their day with other work that relates directly to teaching or promoting literature. Others have full-time jobs and/or childcare commitments and write long hours through the night or at weekends. They are employed across a wide spectrum of occupations: teaching at all levels; television, radio and press journalism, including photography; secretarial work and public administration; nursing and working with those with mental handicap; in military service or farm labouring. Poets from the Nicaraguan poetry workshops, for example, began writing poems as they became literate, the former being taught as an extension of the latter. I cannot now recall a single poet who was not self-supporting, few if any being in a position to subsidise their skills with inherited wealth or at their husbands' expense.

In assembling this anthology, it soon became clear to me that poetry was no longer the prerogative of one class or tradition, and that there might be as wide a variety of poets as there were women. The biggest divider is literacy and language, and it is a major regret that I was unable to seek out sufficient oral poetry from along the Atlantic Coast (where it has the rhythm of music and a strong Black Caribbean flavour) and from among the indigenous Indian communities of Guatemala (many of whom speak little Spanish but have a rich variety of some 23 languages of their own). In Cuba's 'houses of culture' and in Nicaragua's mass *alfabetisación* programmes, poetry is combined not only with literacy but with integrated cultural studies. Learning to write is closely tied to poetic self-expression, and although themes are not laid down the expectation is that new poets will record what they see and feel. As the Nicaraguan poet Ernesto Cardenal said of the poetry workshops for which he, as Minister of Culture, is responsible: 'The important thing is to get people to be simple and specific. If they want to refer to a tree or a bird, to say what *kind* of tree or bird. Beyond that, there can be no rules as to subject matter: if people want to write about love or politics, describe a landscape or review their childhood memories, it's up to them.'

The diversity of poems included here bears this out. With the exception of such established 'senior sisters' as Alaíde Foppa and Claribel Alegría, trained in a classical poetic tradition before breaking free to find their own voice, nearly all the poets are under forty and their work is in the main from their most recent publication. None the less, there cannot be a writer who declares herself free of poetic influences. As well as poems dedicated to twentieth-century Latin American poets (Dalton, Guillén, Neruda, Paz, Mistral) there are many references to the classics of world literature (from Kafka and Dostoevsky to Pound and Whitman). And alongside the collectivising influence of political activism there is that of psychoanalysis, particularly evident in the work of Luz de la Vega or in a poem like Claribel Alegría's 'Confession'.

The section of the anthology called 'Roots of my Song' collects some of the native and national influences as diverse as pre-Columbian mythology and the rhythms of the rumba and calypso. In bringing this variety of sources to birth as poetry, the poets interviewed frequently mentioned a matrilineal tradition that runs from pipe-smoking Indian grandmothers (Ana María Rodas) to the oft-repeated 'interest, sincerity and support of my women friends' (Carmen Matute).

It is a European tendency to wish to define Latin America as a whole, which slides too easily into what I suspect is a racist inability to differentiate between the Americas. While to Latin Americans there are sharp differences between Central America, the Southern Cone, the Andean countries, Brazil and the Caribbean, we tend unthinkingly to follow the United States presentation of itself *as* America rather than as *one* of the Americas.

For this collection I have chosen to follow a political rather than a geographical definition of Central America. Within the region the two words are frequently conflated into the term 'geopolitics', implying the United States' pursuance of self-interested 'development policies' in the area. Panama and Honduras were excluded for lack of available contemporary material. Mexico has, by contrast, such an abundance of contemporary writing that it was eventually excluded as deserving an anthology to itself. The one poem still included here, by Isabel Fraire, is composed for the assassinated Guatemalan writer Alaíde Foppa. Within the region, shifting geopolitical alliances are formed and dissolved, as with the recent Contadora and Peace Plan initiatives. Mexico is sometimes regarded as being in the northern part of the Americas; Panama as entering South America.

Of those here included, Cuba is perhaps the most unusual, being unarguably in the Caribbean. Yet Cuba herself looks to Latin America at least as much as to her neighbouring (and predominantly English-speaking) islands, and has much in common racially and culturally with the Caribbean coastlands from the Yocatán peninsula down as far as Venezuela. A mere 90 miles from Florida, the 1958 Revolution here seems at a reasonably safe remove from unwelcome US attention. After an extended period of cultural orthodoxy, Cuba is again opening to new influences and ideas and generating fresh and outspoken artistic expression. While much of this is undertaken in a revivifying spirit, there is also sometimes a sense of rueful *autocrítica* (self-criticism), as several of the poems here express.

Costa Rica preserves a precarious neutrality, ostensibly assured by the disbanding of its army in the 1940s, but more recently brought into doubt by the presence of US-backed Contra forces based on its territory. Guatemala, particularly since the advent of her first civilian president in over 30 years in 1986, also seeks to promote a neutral image. But while President Cerezo tries to whitewash the genocidal reputation of decades of CIA-instated military rule and propagandise itself as the cradle of the recent Peace Plan, internally the armed forces maintain a reign of the utmost brutality and terror.

Adjoining Guatemala's south-eastern border is El Salvador. Since 1979 the country has been in the throes of a civil war that shows no sign, like Guatemala's, of going away, however ruthless the repression. While the guerrilla movement in Guatemala seems to have dwindled to tiny grouplets holed up in the interior jungle, in El Salvador whole departments are under the direct control of the Revolutionary Democratic Front (FDR), the political arm of the Farabundo Martí National Liberation Movement (FMLN) insurgents. The war has been raging with continuous intensity for nearly nine years, and despite the inauguration of civilian President Duarte in 1983, the military retain effective control, backed to the extent of $2m. daily by the United States.

South-east again of El Salvador lies Nicaragua, where the Sandinista government has been in power since the popular revolution of July 1979, reaffirmed by elections held in 1984 and monitored by international observers. This does not, however, prevent a democratically elected government from coming under daily attack from the US-supplied Contra forces simply for the geopolitical crime of being in what Reagan is pleased to call his 'back yard'.

In editing this collection I visited each of these countries, collecting poems and interviewing many of the authors. The women members of the El Salvador Solidarity Campaign Cultural Committee who shared the translation and selection of the anthology also either come from or have visited the region. It was vital to make this personal contact since little of the poetry included here is available in Britain, still less in English translation. As for the poets themselves, all were pleased to be canvassed for inclusion. Many added recommendations as to translation – particularly Black Cuban poets who rightly felt that many of the Yoruba (or, in one case, Angolan) references might otherwise be lost on English readers.

Women in Cuba, in the revolutionary struggle in El Salvador and in Nicaragua would no doubt echo the words of Nicaragua's vice-president, the author Sergio Ramírez: 'To defend our history is to defend our Revolution . . . We have the past and the present as our constant lessons in the meaning of imperialism.' There isn't a poet included here who can be unaware of what these daily lessons are. Historically, links with Spain and with slavery are still a conscious part of this culture but there are also a surprising number of imperial links with Britain.

It is a commonplace to say that in the past 50 years the United States has done more to destroy indigenous culture than the previous 500 years of European colonialism. Ownership of vast territories by transnational corporations like the United Fruit Company or the oil magnates has forced labour mobility and the breakdown of family structures on whole nations as surely – and sometimes no less brutally – than apartheid in South Africa. Land is still a more fundamental stock-in-trade here than the money economy, and the land, its rites and festivals, the roots it provides and the respect it commands, is a theme often recorded in poetry. Love of homeland, whether of a native community, of one's country or of distant roots in Africa, is basic and unashamed. It figures as large as the passion expressed for a lover.

Even in the post-revolutionary societies of Cuba and Nicaragua, women have not achieved a real equality with men. What is immediately outstanding is how many more professionally prominent women there are here than in many Latin American countries. But, as the poets here reiterate, public recognition does not automatically grant personal liberation. The burden of the 'double day' is the stuff of most women's lives, taken up in work outside and within the home. The only reprieve for the privileged few is still to invoke the assistance of other women, as relatives, neighbours or servants, rather than the equal sharing of chores and childcare with men. Some women regard their situation with a kind of tough resignation, Georgina Herrera (Cuba) going so far as to say: 'If a woman ceases to write poetry because she has children, then that woman is not a poet.' Others, however, refer to 'silenced voices'; discussion of the oppression of *machismo* is open and ubiquitous. Even so, many of the women here included remain generous towards the sacrifices of their male *compañeros*, both in terms of their greater contribution to the military defence of their countries and – more obliquely – the abnegation of a different sort of vulnerability that *machismo* demands. As Michèle Najlis bluntly expresses it: '*Machismo* castrates men of their sensitivity.'

Gioconda Belli, a fellow Nicaraguan and perhaps the greatest love poet of the region, puts it more delicately. 'A woman becomes isolated in the privacy of her home. But the minute she steps outside she becomes a social being, has the support of her sisters – and of our system. We have to fight *machismo* most of all in personal relationships, for the liberation of men as well as of ourselves.' While overtly lesbian poetry is published in Mexico, I have yet to see any in the rest of Central America. As a major area of struggle is against a monolithic external enemy (the United States) women cannot afford to adopt a separatist stance against the male half of their population. In addition to those countries being continually threatened with the military might of the United States and its paid mercenaries, there are others divided against themselves by civil war where the US presence is manifested in massive subsidies to corrupt régimes. It is significant that the poetry of El Salvador, a tiny country where civil war has raged longest and bloodiest, is among the most painful in this book.

Given the magnitude of this type of repression, and the imperative to form a united resistance to counter military aggression, women more often seek to reform rather than reject their men. This produces some radically different demands in terms of women's liberation from those we are used to in the West. For if *machismo* is a strong force in Latin American society, then so equally is the extended nuclear family. Within this context men have strict expectations but also strict obligations. Even in countries where the state is very close to being seen as 'the popular voice, the people's power' it is not looked to to provide what we here would regard as basic welfare services. Instead of demanding child benefits and maintenance, feminists campaign for laws obliging fathers to legitimise their children, to recognise their 'abandoned wives', and to make a reasonable level of payment available. The legally enforced Family Codes of Cuba and Nicaragua stipulate that fathers should contribute a minimum third of their income to any 'abandoned children' and seek to remind men that polygamy is still polygamy even in offering a 'permanent commitment' to successive common-law wives. In Costa Rica Social Security legislation specifies that the head of the family (in practice, the man whenever there is one) should be responsible for supporting the older as well as the younger generation. There are few old people's homes in Central America, and Westerners are generally regarded as remiss and disrespectful for abandoning their parents to the untender mercies of the state. While poets lament the infidelities and betrayals of male lovers, feminists vociferously denounce men who fail in their commitments to their family and society.

In our eyes this amounts to a reactionary view of the family and a Victorian approach to sexual morality. However, rather than develop a 'them and us' attitude in which Western women can criticise their Latin sisters for their expectations of men and we can be greeted with horror for the fragmentation of our family and social structures, the point is, surely, to be able to look at and understand, in this instance through women's writing, how women's individual and social lives shape both their politics and poetry.

Throughout the poems translated here the sharp edge of politics also intrudes. If *machismo* oppresses, distorts and sometimes destroys personal lives, then its institutionalised and militarised form does so on a massive scale. The poetry bears the edge of constant danger, and the anger and despair danger generates. As Roberto Góchez Sosa, father of the murdered student poet Delfy Góchez Fernández, explained to me: 'To write in this country is to vote for one's assassination. To be a writer in this world is to take a risk. To become one in Latin America means becoming a problem. And in El Salvador it is to commit suicide.'

It is not only in El Salvador that the armed forces effectively control the means of communication, and to publish one's writing is to put oneself in the firing line. All the countries included operate a system of censorship which in turn leads to an atmosphere of self-censorship, wherein writers know what may or may not appear, and what the possible consequences are if it does. The statement that the personal is political hardly needs to be made; not one poet interviewed considered being apolitical was a feasible still less an advisable option. There are those who, like Luz Méndez de la Vega in Guatemala or Ana Istarú in Costa Rica, take up the issue of sexual politics. There are others, like Jacinta Escudos or Claribel Alegría in El Salvador, who support the military overthrow of their puppet government. And there are many from Nicaragua and Cuba who fought for the liberation of their countries from other US-backed dictatorships.

In the West to choose apoliticism is a way of passively assisting the status quo. In Latin America the status quo is far more precarious, overshadowed by the threat or reality of US intervention and the military repression that so readily go hand-in-hand. Poets who are not too impatient of being questioned about their political involvement to state the obvious agree with Vidaluz Meneses: 'You have to be in the midst of life to understand it. A poet's rôle is not to stand like a commentator on life's sidelines but to create out of experience.' The price such a poet has to pay for her involvement can be a high one. In Vidaluz' case it has meant separation from her father and children. While refusing to be an observer has spared her (and her poetry) from becoming 'cynical and ironic', sadly she admits that 'my life is a permanent rupture, only in my poetry is there reconciliation'.

This anthology is intended as an introduction to some of the considerable diversity of writing being produced by twentieth-century Central American women poets. The poets here have their own unmistakable songs to sing. But many, while having their own definitions of liberation and feminism, would agree with Luz Méndez de la Vega: 'To be conscious of being a woman is to be a feminist, you can't separate the one from the other. And if you are also a poet, then you are committing that standpoint to print, for others to share.'

Amanda Hopkinson
July 1988

Translator's Note

This anthology was effectively translated not only by a group but by a committee, so perhaps 'Translators' Note' would be more appropriate. The genesis of this somewhat unusual way of translating was due to the involvement of members of the El Salvador Solidarity Campaign Cultural Committee, who shared in the selection and the editing of the book. I would like to acknowledge the work of translators Clara Allen, Imogen Forster, Chris Hudson, Jenny Subow and Susan Thursfield, and the additional help of Anne Wright, members of the El Salvador Solidarity Campaign, and the poets themselves.

In offering this collection, we make no pretence of it being either objective or comprehensive. We have included poems which we admired and felt worked in translation, and a few which were enormously hard to convey without the economical grammar of the original, but whose poetic power not even translation could destroy.

The numbers of us working together and able to meet on a given day made the reaching of unanimous choices and decisions difficult at times. Few poetry translations can have been agonised over by so many for so long! But each of our contributions was valid and working together was an experience we not only learnt but also gained considerable enjoyment from. And the anthology has been enriched by the advice of very many writers from Central America, and by the number of us who have travelled there from England to seek out poetry.

Translation of the poems posed many problems. Beyond the widely different ways in which Spanish can be used in different Central American countries, information was continually needed on native words for which there is no common Latin equivalent. Not only do these refer to plants or creatures unknown in Europe but they often hold a symbolic weight within the culture. The Latin term alone for a *malisquat* or a *malinche*, for example, does not explain whether either plant is as common as a daisy or rare as an orchid; whether it is significant as the insignia of a nation or a party or a tribe, the flower of love or of death. Poetry is created by association as much as by definition. Which is, presumably, what led Pasternak to declare:

'Poetry is only tone. If [in translation] you lose the tone, you lose the poem.'

In addition to indigenous (Indian) and imported (non-Hispanic, mainly West African) words and concepts, many Spanish terms used colloquially have layers of multiple meaning unconveyed by an English equivalent. In the main this is due to the far higher level of political awareness that comes from being an emergent nation in a grossly oppressed part of the world. A word like *concientisación*, for example, has three interpretations. It is commonly used to mean the process of consciousness-raising but can also have a moral dimension: the voice of conscience. Neither sense need strip it of its original one, the simple physiological function of becoming conscious. If a single word, then, like *conciencia* can mean conscientiousness, conscience or becoming consciousness, how to choose between them when there is no English equivalent with the same associations? Only familiarity with a poet's work can help explain their selective vocabulary, and in an anthology of over forty poets, that familiarity is hard won.

Less abstract than a word like *conciencia* but again of particular relevance in writing from Latin America, are words connected to the land and the people, often linking the two. Land ownership is such a fundamental issue in the developing world, and in Central America in particular land distribution is a daily matter of life, death and war. The pre-Columbian heritage, which shares with many American Indian peoples an identification of humanity with the environment, has provided words and symbols for trees and places and communities that have the same name-root. In other instances, there can be many names for something with a single English equivalent. Given its importance as a staple crop, for example, 'maize' is given a different name at every stage of its growth, which stages were – and in rare cases still are – celebrated with religious festivals.

Pueblo is a word that comes imbued not only with a long historical association between 'people' and 'place', but with more contemporary political relevance. It can be affectionate or perjorative according to context, meaning anything from 'my people' or 'nation' to a 'mob' or 'the common masses'. It can signify a place, somewhere smaller than a city, a community ranging in size from the smallest hamlet to a hick country town, depending on context. Occasionally the country of origin is suggested by the sense in which a word like *pueblo* is used. A slogan such as 'el pueblo unido jamás será vencido' (the people united will never be defeated) was born of the struggle for socialism in Chile. While this has been adopted in a spirit of international solidarity by other Latin American countries, it is not a phrase that would have arisen naturally in the very different political contexts of contemporary Costa Rica or Cuba.

In Cuba and Nicaragua, countries which have undergone revolution, an extension of the problem arises for the translator. The vocabulary alters; the prevalence of oratory and public response leads to the adoption of chanted slogans charged with the victories of a hard-won and triumphant revolution. *'Patria Libre o Muerte'* ('free homeland or death') or *'Hasta la Victoria Siempre'* ('ever onward to victory') are repeated as timely reminders of military successes and exhortations to greater efforts in the face of still greater privations. It is hard to convey their impact in English, where such phrases can sound simply stilted and archaic. Even a single word such as *presente* becomes virtually untranslatable by virtue of there being no such familiar mass response in our culture. In El Salvador or Nicaragua it is the answering shout of a people to their revolutionary leaders, and the chorus of many songs. In English, we are left with the dutiful 'present', the schoolgirl's answer to hearing her name called at registration, whereas 'here' or 'ready' sound lame, and 'I'm with you' casually devoid of power.

In the attempt to overcome these and similar difficulties, footnotes have occasionally been used for further explanation, and where a title includes a dedication, clarification has also sometimes been offered. Beyond that, it is hoped the poems will speak for themselves and offer an introduction to the vernacular style that is the hallmark of much contemporary Central American poetry.

Robert Frost somewhat cruelly asserted that 'Poetry is what evaporates in translation.' If that were truly the case, we in the English-speaking world would be considerably impoverished. In the face of such discouragement, I take heart from a Latin American, the revered Cuban poet Eliseo Diego. At a workshop on translation in which we both participated during Managua's first international bookfair in July 1987, he concluded: 'Translation is impossible. But then poetry is impossible. And we all know that love is impossible. None of this prevents us from being caught up in it every day of our lives.' In the hope that fresh versions of these impossibilities will be found in this anthology, it is dedicated to all the brave poets whose work appears here.

Roots of my Song

Prologue

Suddenly expelled
from the chorus of clear voices,
already deprived
of the right
to sing solo.

I slung my voice
over my shoulder —
as harsh and husky
as a weapon —
and took myself down paths
haunted by lamentations.

From here, too,
I came to be proscribed,
the faintness of my voice
unable to match
the rising heights, the violence.

Thereafter
I wander
down byways,
my strangled voice
caught in my throat.

Struck forever dumb
I uselessly attempt
to speak, to sing
even to yell,
with idiot gesticulations.

Janina Fernández *Costa Rica*

To Marianella

Reflections

Words are decreed
according to their proper functions.
We harness them.
We squander them.
Words are transformed by historical process
to march in strict formations.
They separate us, they identify us.
It was words and not embraces
that became our bridges and chasms.
Words are:
this, our first catechism.

Poet or Avenging Angel

It is a terrifying matter
to have a poet in the house.
Everything gets turned upside-down:
family life goes out of the window,
silence is transformed to sound,
words are uttered through unopened lips,
no detail escapes unnoticed,
on the contrary each is grossly magnified.
Dialogue is entered into with the dead,
and with the souls of the living.
Reality's knots are loosened
and knitted with imagination.

Stars are stuck to the ceilings
and the house lit by full-moon light.
The elderly are made to hasten their pace,
children and adolescents to stay theirs.

Having arrived, a poet is no longer here,
and leaving, remains a constant presence.

It is a terrifying matter how Rilke's angels
– with their general odour of sanctity
suffusing all they breathe on –
remain convinced that whatever is carnal
                                              is yet supernatural.

Poet

The secrets of the lyre are not enough
any more than symmetrical flights of birds on the wind,
nor rocks, explosions of jasmine,
nor even this restless heart
beneath my hand.

It is so hard to explain to the listener:
I am this . . . us . . .
and I am flooded with what's ours.

Oh fabulous heavens
holding a canopy
of shining jewels!

Oh the dead devoured
by worms and shadows,
attempting to gently surrender
the unfinished trees to me!*

I discover my voice
and speak for the waiting
life of a thousand looks.

I come from a vast silence . . .
from the silence that speaks!

5

*Throughout Central America and the Caribbean there persists a belief that trees
harbour ancestors. Each new infant is dedicated to a native tree, whose qualities
s/he will express in life and to whom s/he'll return in death.

Fragile God

Steeply inclined,
doubled over
weighing
on the earth's
tough crust:
me and my nothing.

Tablets of paradox
with fantasies of flight,
chained to the innermost
atoms
of the rock:
me and my nothing.

A structure emerging
from the sediment
of dreams and solitude,
ambitious for the space
of cosmic itineraries:
me and my nothing.

Fragile, miserable god,
supreme axis of my world,
constructing and destroying
according to whim,
yet disgusted with who I am:
me, my nothing,
and my words.

Black Christ

With his hands
nailed wide before us
how he weeps then laughs
in the pain
of a simple 'No'
issuing forth from heaven:
leaving him
without a land
leaving him
without a home
leaving him
without a mother
leaving him
leaving him . . .

Landscape with Angolan Woman

The world about your head
               and the child on your back

About your head of wind
                  the parched earth
                  the scant rain.

About your head of rain
                  the elegant palm
                  the singing fire.

About your head of fire
                  evil hunger
                  tepid gruel.

About your head of hunger
                  luminous ruby
                  costly jewel.

About your jewelled head
                  flourishes the jungle
                  flees the antelope.

About your head of antelope
                  the baobab reigns
                  the fish is oracle.

About your head of the fish
                  embossed ivory
                  waters of antiquity.

About your head of waters
                  coffee simmers
                  a country is born.

About your head
               woman,
                  about your head
                  of African woman.

The world about your head
               and the rifle on your back.

Black Woman*

I still smell the spray of the sea they made me cross.
The night itself is beyond memory,
not the sea itself could recall it.

I cannot forget my first glimpse of an alcatraz.
The high clouds, my innocuous eye-witnesses.
And I remember my receding coastline, my ancestral
　　　　tongue.

Here I was transported and here I have lived.
Made a beast of burden,
here I was reincarnated.
With the invocation of many Mandinga epics.

　　　　　　I rebelled

My master purchased me in the market-place
to embroider his waistcoats, to bear his son.
This master died at the white hands of an English lord.

　　　　　　I wandered

This land I had known face down in the dust,
the rivers I had been whipped to row.
Under its sun I had sowed and reaped harvests not mine to
　　　　consume.
My home was the slave compound
I dragged the stones to build,
while singing the syncopated rhythms of native birds.

　　　　　　I revolted

In this land I had touched the dried blood
and dessicated bones of others,
indifferent in death to being forced or not to be here.
It was not for me to envisage the route back home.
Was it to Guinea? to Benin? or Madagascar? or Cape
　　　　Verde?

　　　　　　I continued labouring

9

Mandinga refers to the dominant Yoruba slave culture. Antonio Maceo led the
first national armies of liberation against the Spanish in the nineteenth century,
and was noted also for being a brave fighter, a poet and a half-caste.

Rooting myself in my inheritance of song and hope.
Here I built my world.

I took to the hills

I found true independence at the runaways' fortress
and I enlisted with Maceo's forces.

Now, precisely one century later,
alongside my descendants
I left that blue mountain

I came down from the Sierra

To put an end to capitalism and usury,
to the rule of generals and the bourgeoisie.

Now I am: from today what we have and create
is vital and our own.
Ours is the land
Ours the sea and sky
Ours the magic and vision
Ours in equality, as I watch you dancing
around the tree we together planted for Communism.
Its prodigal wood resounds with the future.

Confession

The patio in my house
dawns with the light.

Not a single tree affords us shade
but the vine leaves fall
and shrivel under the sun and later
offer us much-needed calm.

In the patio of my house
there was no space for games or hoops
and no verandah.

It's just a small corner that belongs to me
and to visitors.
This small space
that fingers the depths of a soul
and rustles the memories of solitude.

Memory

When was it?
I don't know.
I'm for navigating
the seas of memory.
Nicolás Guillén

Enfolded
by the old house of childhood
where pine trees stood guard over my dreams
a full bloom
of orchids and memories
marks the slow return
– the atmosphere of sadness
stained violet and timorous –
of the young girl
fragile as the wind
her heavy plaits
circled with imaginary butterflies
and giants of the future
yet
the instant is so soft
so tender
so fragrant
that suddenly I sense
that amid the dynamic of the stars
girlhood dissolves
leaving behind a space vast as a firmament
where I hurriedly bury
the roots of the present.

In the Street, a Light

Standing behind a memory
as though about to surprise it naked,
standing, biting her lips
a tear piercing her eye,
the fragile flutter
of dry leaves scraping the pavement
and the wind coming down from the trees
rippling the fine dust of the flagstones
and lifting her skirt.

One afternoon in distant memory
she saw Doña Erlinda Jiménez,
on whose proud black head,
shining with nobility,
there were always balanced
rounded golden-white cakes
wrapped in a sweet-smelling cloth
and hurriedly placed in a clean bowl.

Doña Erlinda took her bundle
from house to house,
selling her sweet cakes, her sweet hot cakes,
worn like a crown every evening.

We would watch her in the distance,
her dazzling apron a contrast to
the perpetual mourning she wore for her relatives.
The jingling of coins in her left-hand pocket
marked her approach, as we gradually made out her form
displaying the delicacies in her bowl
that we could peep at from our living-room window.

Meanwhile Grandmother would take some change from
        the closet,
open the window, shake out the shiny wrappings
and choose her cakes.

This afternoon, for no reason I was assailed
by the memory of Doña Erlinda in her apron,
her high-pitched voice announcing her wares,
the gold ear-rings dangling from her ears,
perfectly balancing bowl and cakes.

This afternoon my daydreams invaded me,
here in a silent, nameless street,
standing in front of the pharmacy
in the fourth year
of the revolution.

Marisela Sánchez Alfonso *Cuba*

To Haydée Santamaría*

Haydée's House

The house no longer
looked festive.
Its walls battered
by the winds
as the sea paused thoughtfully
at the shoreline
beneath a sun
that threatened eclipse.
The birds gathered in their young
the flowers gazed at one another
as if wondering what to do
while the news
stuck in our gullet
too great to swallow.

*Heroine of the Cuban revolution who died in 1981.

Gioconda Belli *Nicaragua*

The Blood of Others

I read the poetry of the dead
I who am alive
I who lived to laugh and cry
and shout *Patria Libre o Morir*
on board a lorry
that day we reached Managua.

I read the poetry of the dead,
see ants in the wild grass,
my bare feet,
your straight hair,
as you sat hunched through all our meetings.

I read the poetry of the dead
and feel this blood pulsing in our mutual love
is not our own.

The Heat is Rising

The heat is rising.
The vultures will be sated with so much carrion,
with such a smell of blood in the atmosphere.

Someone watches them,
he could be anyone,
perhaps he who went missing months ago.
It's no consolation
to encounter them
'even if dead'.*
(Someone should tear
from these godless monsters
what they cannot swallow.)
Life,
life,
death.

Because you are foreign
you cannot truly know
what it means to live
in fear,
in danger,
within walls pocked by machine guns,
daily asking yourself:
will they kill me today?

You cannot understand
that for us victory consists in
surviving today and today.

And yet I hold so dear
your freedom.

*The phrase used in press advertisements requesting the return of family
members 'disappeared' by the military. The poem was written in exile in
East Germany.

For Eduardo and Helena, who requested a Salvadorean recipe

Little Tamales from Cambray
To make 4,200,000 small tamels *

Two pounds of mestizo cornmeal
a half-pound loin of Spanish immigrant
all finely chopped and cooked
with a packet of ready-blessed raisins
two tablespoons of Malinche's** milk
one cup of troubled water
then fry the conquistadors' helmets
with three Jesuit onions
one small sack of multinational gold
two dragon's teeth
add one presidential carrot
two tablespoons of pimps
the fat from Panchimalco Indians
two Ministry tomatoes
half a cup of televised sugar
two drops of volcanic lava
seven *pito* leaves
(don't get me wrong, it's a soporific)
set it all to boil
over a slow fire
for five hundred years
and you'll discover its unique aroma.

*4,200,000: The population of El Salvador.
**Malinche was the name of the Mexican princess who betrayed the Aztec ruler
  Montezuma to the Spaniards.

Confession

The father confessor peers at me
through tortoiseshell glasses
and a beatific smile.
Hail Mary he pronounces
latching his pitiless gaze
on to my face.
Full of Grace
I reply.
His glasses reflect me
back to myself.
Have you entertained impure thoughts?
I can't remember, I murmur.
He sets the wheel spinning
stretching the tendons
in my feet.
Enough I shout
I can't bear it.
He repeats the question more slowly.
I think so
it depends
I prefer abstractions
to geometric planes.
Reality overwhelms me
I wanted to kiss his lips
I live in hope of miracles.
Another figure enters.
Do you swear to tell the truth
the whole truth
and nothing but the truth?
I swear,
I stammer between groans.
Have you entertained subversive thoughts?
no, I protest, never
the truth
he repeats contemptuously

stretching the muscles
in my arms.
I say yes
I say enough
I swear to tell the whole truth.
I have written two articles
poems
the occasional short story.
I collect phantoms
a tattered dream
that turns into a bomb
and explodes in the sea.
A third man in our cell
swings the light
so I see his eyes.
Loosening my bonds
he says it won't be necessary.
Did you at any time attempt
to seduce your father?
don't be absurd I protest
and feel in my breast
the electric prod.
I admit it
only please stop.
I was always jealous of my mother,
he kissed me on the forehead
I sought his lips.
Did you intend to seduce him?
I only ever managed to kiss them
when they were cold
in death.
Go on
go on
I'm waiting for it
the truth
says the judge,
we want the whole truth.
I make accusations
invent hatreds
stutter

slip up
the wheel stops its moan.
I impaled butterflies
tore the wings
off flies.
Go on
go on
it's the psychiatrist's voice.
I masturbated
in front of the mirror.
I skewered snails.
The truth
the whole truth.
I spied on the nuns
in the toilet.
I chopped up cats.
How long is it
since you last came to confession?
a long time
I'm not sure
it was in my last book.

Chronology

Where the history of our ancestors begins
carve this phrase
upon the lime-washed walls:
My heart was once a burning bird.

When the time of the conquest arrives
draw three mute dogs
frightening away a steed
clad in the trappings of war.

With the advent of neoclassicism
the moment will occur
to deliberately smash the statues
and discover what lies inside.

Romanticism is another matter:
put a frail-petalled flower
within the pages
of every library book.

Let modernism pass
but inscribe
the clouds
the waves
the gusts of evening wind.

And when we reach our century,
our hard, implacable, beautiful century,
forget all previous lessons,
spread the blank page across the damp grass
allow the rest,
the next generations,
to be the ones who give it a name.

Bright Country

Little Homeland

Behind me
a chaos of pale orphans,
swollen-bellied children,
suffering mothers
displaying their offspring
covered in flies,
canny beggars
who pour their lives
into an artificial leg
and into dirty deals.
I pause and shout:
'The sky is collapsing!'
'Darlings,'
exclaims the fat woman
rubbing her neck,
'have you heard the latest news?
Apparently the sky is collapsing.'
At three in the afternoon
the official meeting commences.
I rise to my feet and announce:
'Sirs,
there is only one item
on today's agenda:
the collapse of the sky.'
The director shows signs of agitation.
'I propose,' he states,
'the construction of a safe
beneath the earth.
We must protect our archives,
our valuables.'
The sentinel calls the barracks
with the news.
'All those in campaign uniform
line up!'
bawls the general.

'Raise your rifles and your bayonets
and hold up the sky.'
The day is overcast.
The normal run of activities
is completed.
The butchers weigh out three-quarters of a pound
to the housewives
and charge for a pound,
the spinsters air their hatreds
to pupils in classrooms,
the Don Juans
swagger with their friends
as the maids
burn the dinner
while considering an abortion.
Shortly the coffee shrubs
will produce red berries,
the cane its honey,
the rows of cotton bushes
their fluffy clouds
which will then be converted
into Cadillacs,
into a night out at the Casino,
into the hire of a suite at Cannes.
I sit down at the intellectuals' table.
'What'll we do,' I ask,
'if the sky is collapsing?'
The old radical smiles.
'It's twenty years since I predicted this.'
'And if it were true?'
enquires the youthful hothead
'What'll we do?'
With a gesture befitting
the historic moment
he takes out his pen
and begins writing a manifesto
of artists and intellectuals
on the tablecloth.
It's been days since I went out.
The sky has not collapsed.

The politicians said it would,
and the leaders,
and the generals,
right down to the beggars,
everyone said it would.
For every young sir
there's a pregnant maid
to maintain the status quo.
For every overfed lady
a tubercular worker picking cotton;
for every politician
a blind man with his white stick.
Everything is permitted.
My childish terror.
The public exhibition
of anguish
is a nuisance to people,
gets in the way of business,
frightens children.
Tomorrow I'll go to market.
The psychiatrist prescribed it.
I'll proffer
twopence to a beggar
and experience compassion.

Home

Home was
the colour of pomegranate
the pungent smell of over-ripe guava
the stubborn yellow wild flower
forcing its way
through the creviced stone
to defy the midday sun.
Home was
the lonely monologues
for hours and hours
to drown the tropical storm.
Home was
clear night skies
like black children's eyes
the rhythm of the earth
in everyone's waist.
Home was
the harbour in my grandmother's arms
and the thundering male chants.
Home was
where I have always been
regardless of the years
or distance between.

Watermelon

You occupy a vast
geographical region,
you red and green and generously rotund
watermelon.
If no tropical sun
is there to ripen you,
your hull is filled
with a Mediterranean warmth.
You were born to slake the thirst
of long summer afternoons.
Cut by full moonlight
you enhance the dark skin
and radiantly white teeth
of southerners.
Or painted into the centre
of the canvas
you permit the artist
a dense violet red
pitted with black.

Carmen Matute *Guatemala*

To Luis Alfredo Arango

Your Name, Guatemala

For so long
I've been in love with my country:
with her earthen pots
her Chinautla doves
her calabash drums
her two-tiered *marimbas*.*

A never-ending list
of artefacts
created by the miracle-working
hands of my people:
The Nebaj *huipiles***
those from Cobán and San Antonio Aguascalientes
from whatever tiny distant village.

And I am in love with the poetry
shaped into pottery
her packs of wild dogs
the clay penny-whistles
played by urchins,
butterflies, fruits and birds sculpted from earth.
There are gourds and rattles
painted with rounded mountains
and rocky outcrops,
terrifying masks of the sorcerer,
                the witch
                and the beauty from Tecún.

I could go on.
The truth is that Guatemala
has never featured in my poems.
My country is so crammed with folklore
I could never get beyond
all her quaint 'Indianisms'.

31

*The *marimba* is a native wooden keyboard instrument played with a number of
leather-covered drumsticks.
**The *huipil* is the richly embroidered blouse worn by the Indian women. Every
tiny community signifies its individuality with the different creatures and
symbols in its embroidery.

But today
Juan came to tell me
in his broken Spanish
that little Catalino
was vomiting blood.

It makes me scream
with rage and shame.
A rattle of stones
hit my face
and my tongue
turned to cloth
as I attempted to repeat
the sweet name
of my homeland.

To Fernando

Costa Rica

On the following day we entered an uncharted land,
divided by undulating mountains . . .
a nineteenth-century traveller

I feel my country ripening in my bones
like a beautiful peach.
This strange land, where heroes
are seldom recognised.
Where every one of us possesses
a relative who's a peasant
and another who's an innkeeper.
I taste my country
in a mouthful of her tepid coffee
dodging the downpour.
It still astonishes me that she is here
with open veins.
Her spirit of solidarity
handed down by distant ancestors
should leave you well pleased.
Her modest courtesy
employing concrete deeds
to call her neighbours
in Nicaragua, El Salvador, Chile
'Comrades!'
This is my country
nourished by her farmworkers.
I look to her generous regeneration:
I have no other homeland.

I Sing

I sing
of the flower of the Caribbean
red lily
of fine height
and the ample breadth
of my hammock.
I sing
of its golden petals
white soul
and girlish
resonance.
I sing
of its hymn
to ancient purity
its clear reflection
of the love of liberty.

I was about to Say

I was about to say
it's been three weeks
since we planted the maize

but perhaps
I should put it like this:
the cornfield is to us
a tender and happy place.*
It roots in our soul
in our land,
it lives in our blood
in our hands;
it means life in harmony
with humanity
with the blade
and the hummingbird.

*Throughout Central America the *milpa* (cornfield) is the focus of the seasons and
of religious ceremonies at each stage of its growth, harvest and consumption.

Lilly Guardia *Costa Rica*

A Child has Died

A child has died
in the district
they call Miraflores.*
Only poor children
inhabit
Miraflores.
As someone might
quell pangs of hunger
with dreams of plenty
so this district
is named after flowers,
an attempt to erase,
to evade
the otherwise suffocating evidence
that here one can breathe only
the air of squalor.
The children who escape
Miraflores
are the ones
who die.

*The name means 'look at the flowers'.

Requiem for my Jamaican Cousin*

Death was his only cover
from the disgrace they heaped on him,
the injustice of his lot.

Without the dignity of understanding why,
he was never permitted
to sing the National Anthem,
his arm raised in salute.

His sweat freely watered
one miserable patch
of unwelcoming and fertile tropical soil
of which my Jamaican cousin
was always denied possession,
as he was always denied
a homeland.

Around and around
white papers circulated
through white hands.
They needed only to state:
'I am a rural black
from the Valley of the Star.
I am a black star
in the whining blue white and red
firmament of our flag.'

*The author, a Costa Rican Black from the Atlantic Coast, was cultural attaché to
Jamaica following Independence in 1962. While some of her forebears had been
brought to work the banana plantations around Limón, others had remained in
the Caribbean.

We are the Nation of Threes

We are the nation of threes:
three great mountain ranges;
three colours to our flag;
three races intertwined;
speaking three languages;
governed by three powers;
three women to each man;
three children to a typical home.
We have three Gods with three voices;
three national dishes, even
three national lifestyles.

We are the nation of threes
and of the third world.

Valiant Homeland

Homeland
of once-clear skies
— now overcast —
of troubled seas and thundering rivers;
of pregnant dawns
and bloodstained sunsets.

Homéland
of strident clamours and menaces
of winds wreathed in mourning
blowing from the North
extinguishing laments.

Homeland
of battles and love
of interminable work
that tires without respite.

Homeland
still born each day
in the pale jade cradle of your hills,
in the clear bright mirrors of your lakes,
in the endless heroism
of your children,
in their fierce unbroken will.

Before you,
bloody, broken
and valiant homeland,
I kneel in reverence . . .
render you this day my homage,
trapped between torment and hope!

Life is So Short

Life is so short.
At every corner,
every turn,
death leaps out at us:
we die at the speed of light.

Life is the dream
from which we are woken
by the sound of gunfire.

The men stay the same,
the mistakes stay the same,
death stays the same.
Only the names
and slogans alter.

In my country
time is measured in corpses:
it's now five-dead-to-twelve,
it's thirty-dead-past-four . . .

Distance does not exist.
So many ghosts have joined the parade
that hand-in-hand
they circle the world,
they join the furthest point
to the country they call
'the land of smiles' . . .
(Do the dead smile?)

My longings amount to this:
the mystery of the world
is no bigger
than one bean.

The *quena* and the *charango** strike up:
the dance of death begins.

*Originally Andean instruments: the *quena* is a flute, the *charango* a small
five-stringed guitar.

Everything is Normal in our Backyard

In spite of the sun
the air
the doves
the inquisitor continues
tending his roses
removes weeds
stones
gnarled roots
turns the earth over
takes a look
rakes
looks again
avoids treading there
the marchioness as always
is doing her crochet
each time someone passes
her glasses slip off
delicate changes in tone
indicate rank
the lonely man dances
yearning to smash his shadow
into a thousand fragments
the one they crucified
is growing old
his prophecies
no longer heeded
the iconoclastic clown
goes over to him
puts a cigarette
in his mouth
have a drag boss
have a drag
but he spits it out
and the squatting beggar

picks it up
the clouds shimmer
the scent of jasmine rises
along the walls
the gaoler
walks by dressed in white
looking for his friend
the priest
the hangman has arrived
and it is time
check
declares the general
his partner starts
with fright
he blocks it with his bishop
mate
the general fires
the victim
topples headlong
I leave the inquisitor
squashing maggots
everything is normal
in our backyard

Life Looks Different . . .

Life looks different through a pane of glass,
it offers distance, protection, isolation

From my window on the twentieth floor
people are insignificant and the landscape is magnified

Here, behind the closed windows of my Mercedes,
I can drive undisturbed through the market with my loin of
    beef

Through Rayban sunglasses, I watch as a tourist watches,
barefoot peasants and women weaving rush baskets
so picturesque

My high window boasts a fine panorama
a distant and sleeping city,
no voices, smells or irritating sounds

Brother: yesterday I shattered your pane of glass
forgive my daring, my fury, my pain, my rage

But that pane was separating us
for you couldn't really see me, hear me, touch me

I broke the glass walls of your car
to let you smell the sweat of my brow, my body

To allow you to see the warts on my peasant hands
and hear my children's cries of distress

It's true it was an act of defiance – using a machete,
a hammer to smash a windscreen. I watched it break to
    smithereens

Then you could see in close-up that I'm not in the least
    picturesque
that I'm only twenty-five and have no front teeth

And that there's a scar scored across my cheek, a
        consequence of
the liquor you sell me, a run-in with the National Guard
and of the dog's life I lead

Brother: I am flesh and bone like you,
touch me, feel my heart pounding

I'm not a clay doll from Ilobasco
Don't watch me from a distance, neither hearing nor
        touching

Come among us, mingle with us in the market
look at our children, even masked in dirt are they really
        clowns?

Yesterday I smashed your windscreen
broke into your flat, pelted your property with stones

I wanted to see the face behind the tinted glasses
and for you to see in me what you have made of us all

Don't be afraid, it was not an act of violence but its
        opposite:
to break your window was a desperate act of love

For the two of us to live together
brother: this is our last chance.

On my Return

When I return, when it really happens,
let the *malisquat** trees flourish on every street corner

The pink and pink of their rich blossoms
will find reflection in the cheeks of children

I know I'll find you quite changed: perhaps bearded . . . or
       greyhaired,
and you, I suppose, will lie and say to me: 'But you are just
       the same!'

I know I'll cry with delight as, from high up,
I begin to make out the bumpy contours of my country

Perhaps I'll feel sick, my heart pounding like crazy
longing all in one day to see again . . . it all.

Then take me by the hand as you would a child or some
       inquisitive tourist
show me your town, my street, our land

Read aloud to me your poetry I've not yet heard
tell me the stories, tales, gossip of mutual friends

For when I return, be sure that it all lives:
our hopes, the *malisquat* and the love of old times.

*A flowering shrub.

My Refuge

It is not easy to live in this century of hatred
if we conceal white splendours within our foreheads
and our guardian angel rejects for ever
the human vocation to kill.

Sinister forms extend their dominion
while the unveiling of particular sins
reveals their dearth of elegance.
My basket of geraniums takes light,
surrenders its aroma
and there are still songbirds rising
in the dawn air.

Must I believe that death
is merely a matter of skeletons,
or learn the mythology of the bee
ancient as the making of honey?

I am not concerned with Paris and Moscow
or any city in Gringoland.
I am rescued from bitter vengeance
by a village of people without newspapers,
and know that the treasures of love in its woods
prepare the way for a new Bethlehem
in the next century.

Exile

My life
is endless exile.
My lost childhood
has no home,
my displacement
has no place.
My life set forth
in a ship of nostalgia.
I lived it at the sea's edge
staring out at the horizon:
I thought one day to weigh anchor,
set sail for my unremembered home
but the journey I'd planned
dropped me at a new point of departure.
Can it be that my natural harbour
is love?
Oh arms that held me prisoner
without offering shelter . . .
how I then yearned to escape
from the cruelty of embraces.
Oh fleeing arms
that sought my hands in vain . . .
Incessant flight
and incessant longing for love
that affords no safe moorings.
There is no longer any promised land
to harbour my hopes.

The Awkward Line

Ants stay behind to play in my shoes
in between blades of grass.
A tree coils around itself in idleness.
I rediscover this countryside
shifting sand in long reaches
the descent of a giant pelican
the obduracy of small snails
prepared for death in their quest for water.
No one will come.
There is no one on this beach where day begins.
The horizon is no more than an awkward line.
It has lost itself
it is trying to erase itself   it is gone.

What are you, Nicaragua?

What are you
but a minute triangle of land
lost in the midst of the world?

What are you
but a flock of birds
     gulls
     swallows
     hummingbirds?

What are you
but the roar of rivers
bearing shinily polished stones in your swirl
leaving watery trails through your hills?

What are you
but the terracotta breasts of women
smooth, pointed, menacing?

What are you
but the song of leaves in giant trees
green, tangled, filled with doves?

What are you
but pain, dust, cries at twilight
cries of women, as if in labour?

What are you
but a clenched fist and a ready bullet?

What are you, Nicaragua,
to cause me such pain?

Swallows at the River

The falling rain
wrinkles the surface of the river
and the swallows fly in circles
grazing the water . . .
and with the sky washed clear
they fly upstream.

Love Poem

Oscar, yuh surprise me
assin for a love poem.

Ah sing a song a love fa meh contry
small contry, big lite
hope fa de po', big headache fa de rich
Mo' po' dan rich in de worl
mo' peeple love fa meh contry

Fa meh contry name Nicaragua
Fa meh peeple ah love dem all
Black, Miskito, Sumu, Rama, Mestizo.
So yuh see fa me, love poem complete
'cause ah love you too.

Dat no mek me erase de moon
an de star fran de firmament.

Only somehow wen ah rememba
how yuh bussing yo ass
to defend dis sunrise, an keep back
de night fran fallin,
ah know dat tomara we will have time
fa walk under de moon an stars.
Dignify an free, sovereign
children a Sandino.

Woman in my Time

Woman

. . A being not yet become
the remote angelic rose
courted by poets
not the accursed witch
burnt by inquisitors
not the whore at once feared and desired
not the mother blessed
not the spinster mocked and faded
not moulded into prettiness
not moulded into pettiness
not living by permission of others
not living according to the demands of others
the she who says, 'Yes!'
to the quest of discovering
the beginnings of her existence.

The New Woman Speaks

Like an obstinate bee
I explore ineffable kingdoms
unknown to you
and, entering your heart's memory,
I mark the virgin places.

Here is eternity
modifying our every moment!

I cannot be the abyss:
the light weaves vines
and broom.

I belong to the bareness
of my language
and I have burnt silences and lies
knowing how I transform
the history of motherhood.

Woman.
Only woman.
Do you understand? . . .
No little bird homing to its nest
nor fodder for animal desires,
nor bluebell woods where the sky becomes lost,
nor witch with her diminutive demons.

Oh, the powers of men
forcing the mutation
of our delicate faces!
Oh, the splendour hidden in my sanctuary
beneath the guard
of intimate angels!

Will my love manage to tell you
I seek a lover
crowned with immortality?

Mother Peace

Three stars
etch your name
mother of our bread,
of our land,
whose outstretched hand
holds our future
as wide as the open sky
flocked with uncaged birds.

We feel you flow in our veins
our blood calls to you
to save us from the shiver that runs
through the spine.

You,
our shelter,
flowering spring,
poem drawn from a smile,
song of the dance of the flowers,
luminous twilight.
An end to tears and bloodshed
to the searing torment of death.
For you I still wait,
a young girl
clothed in love and light.

If I were to Tell my Friends

If I were to tell my friends
that I am my mother's mother
I know for sure
They would never believe me,
but if I explained to them
that this is the most beautiful birth I have ever known,
that I have been nurturing it like a poem,
that at night I have laid her to sleep
explaining the evolution of humankind
while she laughs like a real child
at the monkeys' tale.
That after the literacy campaign I showed her
how to make sentences connect
and that the world is round.
I taught her to love Communism
when I left for Havana
and she did not see me return
with a child in my arms,
only with many in my heart.
Then at last, I am sure,
that if I told my friends
I am my mother's mother
they would believe me.

Mother

With you I shared
pain from the start of time
learning in your laugh
the happiness of spring.
I inherited your long silences
that nurture dreams,
and a heart whorled like a snail
linking me tight
to all humanity.

Last Postcard to my Father,
General Meneses*

Today would have been your birthday
but you are no longer here, for your own good.
I cherish your last words,
your anxiety about my future,
for history prevented you
from witnessing this great moment,
still less from understanding it.
The verdict was already given.
Let me tell you that I hug to myself
your generous love for me.
Your hand holding the spoon
feeding your grandchild that last breakfast,
relieving the heavy atmosphere
of farewell.
Each one ranged on their own side
like two ancient and noble knights,
embracing before the final duel.

56

*Vidaluz's father was with Somoza's hated National Guard, known for its
atrocities as well as ruthless political oppression. With the triumph of the
revolution, he fled to Guatemala to escape the popular demand that all guards
should be tried for human rights abuses and/or criminal activities. But he was
captured by The Guatemala guerrilla movement, tried by popular tribunal,
sentenced to death and shot.

Death of the Parents

Father of Creation to all living illusion
what agony between Your canons and those of humanity.
My father — father of my blood and bone — chose
to escape Thy glittering Kingdom
through ten years of anguish and alcohol.
To be followed long after
by the woman who gave birth to me one dawn
and who swallowed a capsule with the aroma of bitter
    almonds.

I am a consequence of this coupling of royal corpses, of this
    partnership.
I found a stage doorway
through which to escape the jaws of the hounds
You set upon me.
I no longer die the death You decreed
against which I rebelled.
Nor will I enter the trap of destroying myself
in order to live.

Your hounds have bitten so deeply
I no longer fear them.

It is for me to lead my simple life beyond the bounds of
    Your Universe.

Childhood Games

Naked, utterly naked
before your years
of anguish, of silence.
My body cannot cover
all your pain.
I remain naked.
Naked I remain.

Maura Echevarría *El Salvador*

From my Childhood

My childhood is the memory of a patio in Seville.
Antonio Machado

My childhood is the presence
of a hideout in the eaves,
the blue window
framing the sky,
an airy little patio
splashed with geraniums
where my mother beamed
carnation smiles.

My childhood is the rustic
and passive small town,
the narrow street leading to my school.
A park where a tropical landscape
dreams in the afternoon
with kids running races
and teenagers in rowdy crowds
and the paper moons
about an evening dancefloor.

My childhood is my Sunday best
so conspicuous in the packed church.
The communion host held
with my breath.
A Madonna lily extending
her innocent grace
and the Nazarene opening
the doors to faith.

My childhood is a thin thread
of honey and bitterness.
My infancy has the look
of another childhood in flower

It's the memory moored
in tiny ports
where my song
blooms with a living presence.

Gioconda Belli *Nicaragua*

Maternity

My body
like a welcoming country
obligingly stretches.

And the plains of my belly
assume the form
of rotund pulsing slopes.
While inside,
in who knows what mystery
of water blood and silence,
like a fist slowly unclenching there grows
the child you have sown
in the curve of my fertility.

Yesterday's Child

You were a child of the mists
almost ethereal;
you gave my smile a name
drawn from my soul.

You were
an angelic sailor
of many voyages
coursing my blood.

You grew as the lily,
and as the algae;
in your depths was born
the dawn.

And reaching new seas
turbulence
staked your strength
with living masts.

Meadow of clean snow
forest of cries!
And you, sweet seed
so firmly planted.

Hidden in my pulse
without surrender;
throbbing in the fears
of my unfathomed depths.

You sought form and words
from within my breast;
you chose your expression
from among my ancestors.

You emerged from the tower
of ages
and signalled
to future moons.

Don't think I'm telling you
fairy stories:
if you don't believe me
reach for this teardrop.

My Daughter at the River

From the riverbank
I see Christian, my daughter,
standing upright on the punt
stretching out her neck,
holding out her arms.
Suddenly, like a queen of the world,
she turns a pirouette on the green
lawn of the river and tumbles.

Cony Pacheco *Nicaragua*

Just Like María

On the beach I study
the shapely legs of my friend Marina.
I think: will María's legs be like that?
If I see the soft eyes of my niece Johanna,
I think: will María's eyes be like that?
If I see the neat figure of some unknown girl I think:
will María's body be like that?
When I look at my naked breasts and run my palm
around their contours I ask myself:
will María's breasts be like this?

To my Son

I thought I saw you,
heard your laugh.
I've seen you so serious, so solemn,
heard your little voice tremble as you ask:
'Are you leaving again?
Are you going back to the mountains?
Is this what defending our country means?'

You are only six yet already you know how to shout:
'War's not a game.
Training's not a game.'
Then you ask: 'Why is there a war?'
Too young to understand
that you yourself are the reason.

This is how I love you.
Because you are my son,
but most of all because
you are the future.

Orlando

I remember you, my son,
brave and daring,
hoarse from shouting so loud on demonstrations,
in your brown striped T-shirt,
the one we keep in the second drawer.

Phone Call from my Mother

Hello, daughter.
How are you?
Thank heavens
for the sound of your voice.

Do you know what?
I felt as though my soul was hanging by a thread:
I heard on the radio
that at daybreak
some buses were blown up,
bombs were set off,
and a round of machine-gun fire
raked the lives of young and old.
And all of this, little light of my life,
right by where you live . . .

Don't worry on my account,
my old aches and pains
aren't significant.
Knowing you are well
is the best possible medicine.

A spray of roses
teases the colour into my cheeks,
and I feel like an architect
and I feel like poetry
thanks to the simple miracle
of always being able to count on my mother.

Lovers
and Comrades

Julia Chavarría *Nicaragua*

The Letter

When I took your letter
in my hand, I couldn't tell
whether to read it or not.

Salvador

You smile the smile of a youth

as you softly pluck your guitar
and we remember
those tense moments we lived through in 1978
when, together with Martha and Alicia,
we would strike up protest songs in the church
that was only a few short metres past
the Fifteenth Division of Police.

Then your voice was still a child's.
Now,
youth of the Revolution,
you sing on with more devotion than ever.

You become so absorbed in each song
you appear to forget that facing you
there's someone listening.

When you finish
you remain rooted to the seat
still gently plucking your guitar.

When a Woman Doesn't Sleep

When a woman doesn't sleep
the magic escapes from her breasts
and her wakefulness should be as feared
as a myth slowly spreading
between reverie and night.

The time for spells and spirits passes.

Silence fills once more with sweetness
straw hats reappear with summery weather
sun and clouds effect a reconciliation.

But the atmosphere retains the threat of eyes
chasing the night stars.

Last night I didn't sleep and you should beware:
you could be in for a dread awakening.

Huntress

Mountain animal, I am bound to pursue you
watch for you in hiding
hunt you down with poisoned arrows
track your footprints
find your lair

corner you
and trap you there

the patient huntress
to make of you
prisoner   victim   prey
mine only mine
to devour

or perhaps to free
should that fear in your eyes
touch
the stone that is now
my heart.

And . . .

. . . so the pretext to repeat your name
surfaces in the wet night,
humid and tender
as a wide-open flower
with trembling petals
which enfolded and drew me
deep into sleep,
a dream of etching your name
in every corner I have ever lived
or have yet to live
until the wind
carries me on like a seed
to bloom in uncharted lands,
perhaps to be reborn as the girl
listening to stories
in evenings reminiscent of Nicaragua
where the scents of the newborn earth
weave in her entrails
the green life of the luxuriant tropics
like me, like you,
like the leaves we covered ourselves with
when they wrenched us from Eden's paradise.

A Crescent Moon

A crescent moon
rides between my thighs.

He is the steed with flanks
golden as the sunrise.

The he-dove settles
like a round, ripe plum.

Mated dove that I am
I circle around him.

A black hare
leaps from my lover.

He enters me as I lie
curved as a guava.

The centre of his body
of mine is the centre.

One ebony tree with two branches
one dye coursing through us.

A crescent moon
rides between his thighs.

I am the steed with flanks
golden as the sunrise.

This Net Binds me Tight

This net binds me tight
a Ulysses to his mast
to where a bank of treacherous seaweed
obstructs my line of flight.
My tongue aches with a thirst
not like that thirst wherein I have to seize you
like the blinding hurricane.
No rope can hold me now,
nor can turbid reefs restrain me.
I am a perfect shaft of light,
I burn within a sunflower
delirious with desire.
My blood rises
in an adolescent rush.
I bring a golden orchid
to lay upon your genitals.
No rushing rivers in flood
no saltwater torrents
can longer interrupt my flight.
I'm to drink the sea
you hold within you,
snatch the goblet
filled with milk of the hearth-gods,
the cottony snow
of light-bright sheets.

You cloak your back with the sky.
You between my back and the sky.

Memorandum

It couldn't matter less to me
that you have no house
        no car
        no job
nor that my family considers you a bad lot.
It doesn't matter to me that you are an evolutionary failure
according to masculine genetics
or that you resemble a retrograde ancestor
in the way you survey each woman who passes
with the investigative air of Diego Velásquez
and the conquering spirit of Hernán Cortés.
The thing I really cannot stomach, however,
is your lamentable lack of imagination over loving me:
the horizontal dreariness
following on the proud parade.

Beginnings of Development

Our love has not attained
even the period of transition
and it is suffocating us
with religion.
God willing
       we speak to each other
God willing
       we see each other
God willing
       I am aware we sleep together
       or we sleep together and
       I am not even aware of it.
Thanks to the Christian–Marxist alliance
       I remember you
       I am your neighbour
You must love me as you love yourself.
It is in the interests of development that
       I propose
we move towards unequal dictatorship
towards social democracy
or we risk becoming the negation
of Historical Materialism.

The Heavenly Family

The lampshade is tilted
to illuminate your book.
Your imperious boots
are scrutinising me from the carpet.
Your clothes over the stool
wait for me to hang them.
You serve yourself the prime cut of meat
without a glance in my direction.
The radio station
and the television channel
are tuned by you.
The cinema
or the restaurant
is selected by you in advance.
The day's menu is prepared
by me according to your taste.
I lie sleepless in bed
– motionless –
in order not to disturb your rest.
Your complacent orgasm
takes no account
of my utter exhaustion:
it is irrefutable proof
that you rule
because you're a man
and because . . .
Despite every protest
nothing has changed
between you and he who
emerged from the caves
knowing precisely how to break us in
throwing us behind you on horseback
throwing us down on our backs
against the pillows of our bed
and . . . forever this!   throttling our words
with the weight of a womb
laden with fruit.

Metamorphosis of your Memory

I remember you
then, dynamic
then, handsome
then, whole
then, abundant.

I regard you
now, weak
now, distorted
now, diminished
now, gone.

Ana María Rodas *Guatemala*

Mr Revolutionary

Tonight
you will fail to find me in your bed.
You will, however, find it a little strange
that our love has now been sabotaged,
oh my former master.

You, so concerned with social control,
have shown yourself incapable of noticing
that in your own home
you present the exact model
of the perfect tyrant.

Love Story as Related by One of the Parties

We knew each other well
and we still forgave each other.
You said you loved my long hair
and my habit of reading you verses
which (at the time) you found memorable.
It was later I became too complicated.
I theorised at length
and would not learn to cook.
In short,
you did not get the love you sought.
I still wonder what kind of love you meant.
What re-examination of criteria led you to believe
that love has formulas
and laws enshrined in sayings?
I still wonder what kind of love you meant . . .
It hurts to have exchanged you for words
tonight as I sit down
to theorise with myself
while outside it rains
and you
seated at table in another house
wait for the coffee
that a woman with short hair
is about to serve you.

I Could Have Lived

I could have lived close by you
so sweetly
and lit your reading lamp and seated myself
in the broad armchair comfortable with time.

I could have cut a rose
and placed it on your writing desk
or spent the late afternoon
embroidering a flowery tablecloth.

Something different happened:
the opposite happened:
I wandered far and lonely
– tremendously lonely –
for you did not wish to be my companion.
But in all the comings and goings of travel
these ways have taught me – ah so well –
to know myself!

A Whole Lifetime

A whole lifetime apart from you.
A whole lifetime . . .

Why? . . . Can you explain? . . .

It would have been so beautiful
to gaze at a star
through our window.

So You Never Reply

So you never reply to my letters.
I no longer expect or request anything.

At this late stage it would be absurd
to ask the postman if he has for me
an envelope that glimmers
like a tiny star.

Letter to a Lover

Mapping every inch of your skin
I forgot the contours
of my land.
I abandoned wandering its roads,
I ignored its hunger and violence,
submerged in a constant spasm.
So I turned myself into a snail,
into a tortoise,
hiding in the depths of my house.
I lived out my useless existence
singing like the cricket in the fable.
My home lacked doors and windows,
its shell my sarcophagus
walled with self-obsession
enclosing me in its chrysalis.
None the less our love continued growing.
Our love that has become
a dialogue of years,
tempered with kisses,
blows and bites,
and an enormous bread-basket
for sharing with everyone.
Today beneath our sheet
every woman, man and child
of our people is taking cover.
Let us establish
that from now onwards
there's room for everybody!

Island

I have been nothing
I am no one
but a lost island
without birds
or inhabitants
without living voices
a wasteland
barren
a dark island
orphaned
without tenderness without shelter
a place of petrified cliffs
no smiles
nor honeycombs
I am a harsh island
a deep remote lament
cornered in the wind's solitude
dust and salt
nourish my being
prayer and hope
are exiled
without far stars
without an oracle
namelessly
I the torture victim.

Rosario Murillo *Nicaragua*

To Daniel*

It Hurts

It hurts,
the pain of evening falling about my shoulders
the absence of your touch in the dark,
memories holding the threat of rain,
streaming from all directions
penetrating my senseless body with a sadness that leaves
me blind
deaf
abandoned.

Blanca, Like a Giant Lily

Death disappeared today between your eyes
it ceased to matter
it was erased like the dreams of childhood
lost to maturity
or like police gangsters
in some improbable Italian film.
I sent death a letter today, no stamps, no address,
to death I sent a death sentence.

She slipped into her green dress
surprised she shot a last look at the mirrors
and, like one who doesn't know anything,
left for nowhere, without destination,
perhaps she thought, before shutting the door,
that she had left some unknown woman behind her
with a delicious new skin
her hair tousled
between her eyes
her mouth fresh
thousands of dark freckles
and an infinite longing to love
tearing her legs apart.

87

*Her husband Daniel Ortega, president of Nicaragua.

To Comrade Blas Real Espinales

I knew Salvador (for that was his code-name)
in Honduran exile. We returned with Laura
to the house where once we'd met.
He was skinny. His eyes were alight
                    and strangely sweet.

The next week he returned to Nicaragua
and fell fighting in Chinandega.

We hardly spoke
                    but I still see
those peaceful eyes so intensely alive
                    in pain,
                    opened
                    in death.

Precisely

Precisely because I lack
the beautiful necessary words
I strive through action
to speak to you.

Ana Ilce Gómez *Nicaragua*

The Goddess of Night

The Goddess of Night speaks to me:
'Your heart will prove as eternal
as my kingdom . . .'
My love, do not open the door
to the dawn.

In the Struggle

Tegucigalpa-Managua

I see you laughing inside your telephone booth
putting on your most cheerful expression:
                    'Everything's fine.'

Seated, long-distance, I discern you
from far away pouring into me
                    all of your anguish.

The Departure

I still vividly remember
that unnatural pallor,
the berets, the frightened eyes.

Outside,
Polo adjusted the olive-green tent
(which at the last minute turned out too short
and we had to pin down the flaps with two planks,
nailed to the frame)

— Polo — who's now dead.

The comrades
filed out
with their new uniforms and their guns
in two neat lines.

(A neighbour came out into the adjacent courtyard)

And Augusto in the cabin
of the truck
waiting for the order
                                to depart

The Departure II

In his yellow shirt
— all ready to get changed —
Augusto was driving.

And when I gave the signal to depart
he drove past saying goodbye
with a smile.

Up There in the Mountains

I left my heart
up there in the mountains
where love of my homeland
and of the revolution
is smelled, touched, felt.
There, where words are irrelevant,
deeds, life, commitment
overwhelm us.

Here and Now we are Building our Future

This memory
can never be erased.
My father was a fighter:
he was often behind bars,
held in solitary, tortured,
every human right denied.
Still his eyes burned with a defiant flame.
I was then only four years old,
I didn't know the way
to the military prison,
everything was so different then.
I was taught about the prison
through taunts and insults.
I don't know how my mother managed;
they let us in to see him in his cramped corner
and he raised his clenched fist
although weak and wide-eyed, unshaven and hollowed,
his mouth swollen and red.

It was then I began to dream of another homeland
and longed to trap a star.

Janina Fernández *Costa Rica*

To Inactive Intellectuals

Inside a wall of books
constructing a lexicon of violence
the theorists design
their exquisite investigations:
Subversion,
Revolution,
Liberation.
Without so much
as stepping outside.

Delfy Góchez Fernández *El Salvador*

It will be my Pleasure to Die*

they are bound to kill me
when?
I don't know . . .
what I do know clearly is that I'll die soon,
cut down by the enemy.

since I want to die in struggle
I will always strive for such a death.

since I want to die alongside my people
I will never cease to be at their side.

since it is our cry that will strike home
I will keep on raising it loud.

since both history and the future
are on our side,
I cannot swerve from this path.

once I join forces with the revolution
all my perspectives and every dream
will be attained.

every action I perform
is a blow struck at the enemy
however it is delivered.

I am now committed.

what is undeniable
is that they will kill me.

and my blood will water our land
and flowers of liberty will blossom.

and the future will open its arms
with warmth, full of love,
to shelter us in its breast.

our mother will laugh with joy
at being reunited with her child, her people,

*This poem was written days before she was murdered on 22 March 1979 by
security forces while taking refuge in the Venezuelan Embassy.

with the child who yesterday begged for a crust of bread
and today swells full as a river.

the mother who was slowly dying
and who now is living the dream she yearned after,
and the eternal militant
whose blood
nourishes the day
that is coming to dawn.

yes, it will be my pleasure to die, full of love.
I wish to die according to the custom of my times
and of my country:
cut down by the enemy of my people.

I am Happy

Today I have discovered happiness.
Today I learnt
it's not that I'm *on* the way
        or *by* the way
        or *with* the way
I *am* the way!

Jacinta Escudos *El Salvador*

To Roque Dalton*

Trick

I couldn't have not been on time
for your funeral.
They say I was really tiny
when you died.
They weren't aware
I watched them all
through the keyhole
and that together we mounted guard
at the entrance to the Planes de Renderos
and that I gave you a kiss
and that now I can speak out:
truly, Roque, you never died.

*Poet and hero of the Salvadorean revolutionary movement, assassinated 1980.

Gradually . . .

Gradually, leaving detail behind, we advance.
We move on freed from absurd obsession
that can only evoke sterile fantasies.

I can leave you my looking-glass.

I hope my name won't appear with the rest
on a list belonging to Colonel This or General That.
No one can imagine the danger. It is too great.
We throw stones at them. The enemy. The vast and
ill-defined enemy, the devilish and unfeeling enemy.

(Guerrillas know how to laugh too.)

Everyone asks if I am afraid. The enemy
knows too much. Perhaps they'll get me with
three bullets just as I leave the airport. Fear.
Fear? Fear.

We grow up with it. Day in day out the same
question: will they kill me today? Fear. In
El Salvador, fear has become a national habit.
Fear. We no longer know what fear is.
Fear is a part of life. You
know better than anyone that fear is part
of your life.

Perhaps I'll be able to remember you, with
your angelic expression, your eyes deep as the sea,
just before dying. Perhaps I'll remember how you
stared at me — like someone trying to wrest
another's secrets with a look; or when you
stroked the hand of that beautiful woman, whose
name I never discovered . . .

It's inevitable to go over these things
before dying. I imagine all of this . . .

In love as we are
with the Revolution.

I am a Mirror

Water glistens
on my skin
I don't feel it
water cascades in streams
down my back
I don't feel it
I rub myself with the towel
I pinch my arm
I don't feel it
back on earth I look in the mirror
she also pinches herself
I begin to dress
in fits and starts.
They break out from corners
lightning shrieks
empty eye sockets
scampering rats
teeth
I still don't feel.
I lose myself in the streets
children with grubby faces
begging me for money
girl prostitutes
hardly fifteen years old
on the streets everyone is victim.
Tanks approach
bayonets are raised
bodies fall
weeping
at last I feel my arm
no longer a ghost
I hurt
therefore I exist.

I look again
running youths
losing blood
women with panic
in their faces
this time it hurts less
I pinch myself again
and now I feel nothing
I simply reflect
what happens
before my eyes.
The tanks
aren't tanks
even the shouts
aren't shouts
I am a smooth mirror
nothing can penetrate
my surface
is hard
bright
polished
I am now a mirror
disembodied
a faint memory
of pain.

Once we were Three

It was winter with snow
it was night
today is a green day
of birds
of sunlight
a day of ashes
and laments
the wind pushes me
it drags me over the bridge
over the cracked earth
over the dry gully
overflowing plastic and tins.
Death takes life
here in Deyá
the gullies
the bridges
my dead lurking
at every corner
the innocuous railings
of a balcony
the blurred reflections
of my dead
smile at me in the distance
they take their leave
departing the cemetery
to form a wall
my skin becomes
transparent
they knock at my door
they gesticulate.
The bridge was stone
it was night
arms linked
to the sway of a song

our breath rose
from our mouths
in little crystallised clouds.
It was winter with snow
there were three of us
today the earth is dry
it reverberates
my arms drop
I am alone
my dead mount guard
they signal to me
they assail me on the radio
in the newspapers
the wall of my dead
is rising
it stretches from Aconcagua
to Izalco.
They maintain the struggle
they mark out the route
the bridge was stone
it was night
no one could tell
how they died
their tormented voices
were jumbled
they died in prison
tortured.
My dead are rising
they are angry
the streets are deserted
my dead still wink at me
I am an expropriated cemetery
they are too many to bury.

The Dead

The dead
will uphold the raised arm of the warrior,
the voice of the people,
the tools of the peasant.

The dead . . .

Who will hold up the hands of the dead?

They Pursued us through the Night

They pursued us through the night
they cornered us
leaving us defenceless but for our hands
linked to millions of other linked hands.
They made us spit blood,
they whipped us;
they subjected our bodies to electric shocks,
and filled our mouths with chalk;
they left us nights on end locked in with wild beasts,
they threw us into timeless dungeons,
they tore off our nails;
our blood rose to the roofs,
covering the level of their faces,
but our hands remained
linked to millions of linked hands.

I am Taut

I am taut
as a drawn bow.
It is proper
I should fire
into the heart
of all matter
without flinching.
I am
surrounded, ambushed.
It is necessary
to confront the enemy
or die
of waiting.

Zaída Dormuz *Nicaragua* *

The Final Offensive

Monday 4 July 1979
no one was at work.
Streets were deserted.
Shops, factories, market,
everything closed.
Only Somoza's National Guard
eyed one another.
Supermarkets were ransacked
(people were hungry).
Little districts, whole neighbourhoods,
then the cities threw themselves into the struggle;
even kids of only eleven or fourteen
like me shouted aloud
'Free Homeland or Death!'

*A twelve-year-old caught up in the struggle that triumphed in the revolution of
19 July 1979.

Patria Libre: 19 July 1979

Strange to feel this sun again
and see rejoicing in streets overflowing with people
red-and-black flags everywhere
a new face to the awakening city
still smoking with burning tyres
still broken up with high barricades.

The wind hits me full in the face
where dust and tears mix freely
I take a deep breath to convince myself that it's no dream
that over there are Motastepe, the Momotombo, the lake,
that at last we made it,
we did it.
So many years of keeping faith come wind come rain,
believing that this day could be,
even after learning of the deaths of Ricardo, Pedro,
      Carlos . . .
of so many others they tore from our side,
eyes they gouged out,
without ever blinding us to this day
which today breaks within our hands.

How many deaths to catch in my throat,
beloved dead with whom we once shared this dream,
I remember their faces, their eyes,
their confidence in attaining this victory,
their generosity in dedicating themselves to it,
certain that this jubilant hour would yet come
well worth the price of death.

It hurts to give birth to this happiness.
It hurts to be unable to awaken them to witness
this great people emerge from darkness,
their faces refreshed and smiles on their lips
as though long kept in storage
and suddenly released, all at once.

Thousands of smiles are emerging from cupboards
in burnt-out houses, from the tiled yards,
smiles brilliant as slices of watermelon,
medlar and guava.

It must be my duty to rejoice again and celebrate
on behalf of my fallen comrades,
indulging in this triumph so much due them,
so much the child of their flesh and blood
and in the midst of the bustle of this bright day,
high up on the lorry,
riding through the streets passing the beautiful faces
of my people,
I wished I could grow arms to embrace them all,
and tell each one how I love them,
that blood has engendered us with its painful bond,
that we are now to learn how to speak anew,
walk anew;
that in this future – a heritage of death and laments –
the loud blows of the hammer will ring out,
the swish of lathes,
the whistle of machetes;
these shall be the weapons
to strike flame from the ashes,
cement, homes, bread from the ashes;
that we will never falter, never surrender,
that like them we will know
how to think of the beautiful days to be seen by others
and in the inebriation of liberty
that takes to the streets, shaking the trees,
and blowing the smoke of fires
let us keep company with

> serene
>   happy
>   ever-living
>   our dead.

Today Fidel Speaks to Us

although we couldn't know
what he was going to tell us
even if it was a matter only
of sensing him there
through the television screen
the house settled into silence
and the doves paused in their cooing.

today Fidel speaks and I have grown,
his fine wrinkles show the passing of time.
I am drawn to his voice
which fills the district
with a familiar calm:
we wait it with bated breath
swift   fleeting
it has become part of our
consciousness
we feel it even when we are absorbed
        by the crowds
– a worker who caught sight of him
at his factory will never forget –
grandmother stores the memory in her bag
along with her lilies and longlost loves.
I understand how
high up in the Sierra
they used his photo as an ikon.
there is only one way to love him:
we have grown in him as within a large tree
for this reason we protect him
with such pride and strength.
today Fidel speaks
my children long for beards and berets
they know nothing of hunger and war
they can't manage a word like Nicaragua
but they'll sit in front of the television
and when they walk through the parks
the streets   to school
they will see him there.

Minimum Homage

With production at an all-time low
without sufficient typewriters or
even desks,
we are taking up the challenge
of the second phase of your work, Carlos,*
and it reminds me of when you took to the mountains
with a few comrades, fewer arms,
and a banner.

*Carlos Fonseca, military commander of the first Sandinista National Liberation
Front, killed in 1976.

Now I Know

Now I know
I'll never be other than one
of love's guerrillas.
I find my place somewhere
roughly on the erotic left-wing.

Loosing bullet after bullet
at the system.
Losing strength and time
in preaching my nocturnal gospel.

Perhaps I'll end up like that other madman
gunned down in the sierra.*

But since my struggle
is of no political consequence to men,
my journal will never seek a publisher
nor will my photograph
adorn their hoardings.

We Stopped at the Crossroads

We stopped at the crossroads
signed for Andrews Salts and Alka Seltzer
in Totonicapán.

Holding hands
we ate the green apples —
How many green apples there have been in my life!

Now the green apple season is over
and at those crossroads
the hoardings spell out
a different message.

*Ché Guevara, killed in Bolivia in 1967.

Certainty

Soon a whole multitude
will echo the clarion call
in gentle tones.
Paul Eluard

Though we should live a hundred thousand years
we would still have the sun's dynamic within us,
as we await the sweet cane harvests of the future
ruffled by butterflies borne on wings of hope.
We are the exceptional witnesses.
We have undertaken the hardest tasks.
We have navigated the Caribbean
on the back of the great Latin American turtle.
The tide will rise high.
And we'll lack neither our daily bread
nor the stars by night.

Time of Awakening

To Julio

Time

I turned over
my past
my future
and all at once
my present
caught light.

For Carole

On the Beach

Oh, it's nothing,

here
hold the bucket with your other hand
I'll tell you a story if you don't cry
the story takes place in China –
do you know where China is?
She shook her head
and approached reluctantly
her nose running
and sand running
from her blue swimsuit.
Once upon a time, I began,
in China,
they bound women's feet
so they couldn't grow
the rest of them grew
only the foot
remained a prisoner
within its bandages
and the poor women there
could scarcely walk.
Their fingernails
were made to grow long
not so much nails as claws really
and those poor women
could hardly lift a cup
to drink tea.
It's not that they were idle,
but that their husbands
fathers
brothers
wanted them like that
objects of luxury
or slaves.

This is still something that happens
all over the world
it's not the feet they still bind
it's the mind, Carole,
and there are women who accept this
and women who don't.
Let me tell you
about Rafaela Herrera
who with drums
with rockets
and with shouts
scared away none other
than Lord Nelson.
Lord Nelson was afraid,
he thought the whole country
was in uprising
as he arrived from England to invade Nicaragua
and returned home again
in defeat.

Your crooked little finger
resembles being a woman
you must use it often
to see how well it works.
Go back and play now
don't carry the sand
help your cousins
in building the castle
give it towers
and walls
and terraces
and destroy
and construct,
keep opening
doors and windows.
Don't carry sand,
let them do it
for a turn
so that they have to bring you, the builder,
buckets full of sand.

Strike

I want a strike we can all join in,
a strike of arms, legs and hair,
a strike born of every body.

I want there to be a strike
of workers   of doves
of drivers   of flowers
of experts   of children
of doctors   of women.

I want an enormous strike
to include even love,
a strike where everything comes to a halt,
the clock   the factories
the workforce   the schools
the buses   the hospitals
the highway   the ports.

A strike of eyes, of hands and kisses.
A strike where breathing is forbidden,
a strike to give birth to silence
          so we may hear the footsteps
          of the departing tyrant.

In the Mountains

Rain, mosquitoes, cold,
the long black night.
The deep riverbed
muddy water swelling to my waist,
open-mouthed fish,
trees groaning with the night,
ghosts leaning
towards the mountain's silent foothills.
The birds' piercing cries
mingled with the river's murmuring voices.
My silence, myself,
my anxiety held with my breath.
My eyes pierce
the night's cold ramparts.
A new day breaks,
a new sun,
a new hope
and me . . . I've grown a little
together with my people
I've climbed one, two, three
steps towards the future.

On to the Promised Land

And we walked for days on end,
crossed whole mountains,
rivers, canefields, bridges,
by boat and helicopter,
until we arrived
ragged and hungry;
they brought me a child
so he wouldn't die on them,
for we were the Liberation Front
and we came to stay.
We brought with us hope
clasped in a strong raised fist,
and with them returned to march
on to our future.

Song of Hope

Some day the fields will be forever green
and the earth will be dark, sweet and moist.
Our children will grow strong and tall in this land
and our children's children too . . .

And they will be as free as the trees and birds
of our native hills.

Every day they will awake to rejoice in the gift of life
in the knowledge that this land was won for them.

Some day . . .

Today we plough the parched fields
but every furrow is watered with blood.

Deus

Nothing is superfluous,
neither the dragonfly nor the petal.

Nor are we purposeless
in our perfection and beauty.

And in the space within the space
of every fleeting word
there is no room for error.

The golden mean establishes
every revolution of the wheel.

Nothing exists in excess or dearth.
Each of us has within:
Serpent and Eagle,
the venom of every epoch.

And humanity is grateful to be
generating her work, while its creation
recreates humanity.

Nourishment of light.
Nourishment of work.

Give thanks for your mortality.
Take solace in your transcendence.

Prayer I

Give me, Lord,
a deep silence
and a thick veil
over my face.
Thus may I become
a sealed world,
a darkened island.
I'll painfully excavate myself
as through hardened earth,
to reach my furthest depths.
Once I'm bled white,
my life will become
lithe and clear.
Then, like a sonorous and translucent river
my trapped song
will flow free.

Prayer II

So pious and so cruel,
your hand
forever separates me
from the easy way.
You injected bitterness
into a ripe fruit,
a complaint
into what might have been
the full cup
of happiness.
A deep shadow
extinguished the birth
of my joy.
Oh hidden voice,
of unanswerable demands,
oh exacting God,
who laid such a rugged bedrock
as the foundation
for the pensive course
of this life.
I am not worthy
to have so much asked of me
nor that in my failure to respond
you will not extend
your helping hand.

A Christmas Poem for Alaíde Foppa*

I

here we sit   wordless   tearful
          hoping you'll show up   knowing
we'll probably never   see you   again

scanning the papers for news of you
      we see old photographs
how beautiful you were!
                    (I didn't know you were so beautiful)

they were taken many years ago
      yet already
          depth and sadness mingled
      with a woman's beauty
                    exceptional and splendid

a beauty that over the years   faded   gently
          ever more blurred
      more tender   and intimate
          less clearly etched
like the pattern waves leave on the sand
      gradually more eternal

already the bullets graze our skin   though they're still
      far away

we catch ourselves speaking of you in the past tense
and bite our tongues
and look for your face in the mirror

II

but in the mirror   we don't find your face
only our own
or one that looks like ours
or one we'd like to have

124

---

*Alaíde Foppa, disappeared, presumed murdered by Guatemalan security forces
in 1980.

there is never any other face in the mirror
only one face we always examine
  with intense concentration
  in the mirror of the other faces
  which float above shoulders
  above the scarf the pearl necklace
    the turtleneck sweater
      the silk blouse

  we never see any other face
    but our own

  that is the face we miss when yours is missing
but there are many other faces
          many

III

did the chauffeur who was kidnapped with you have a
  face?
  does he now have a face?
  if we had seen him would we know his face?

no one ever looks at chauffeurs
  at secretaries who smile mechanically
   over the typewriter
  responding to mechanical smiles
   of people who never really look at them
     or if they do
        don't see them

  secretaries chauffeurs waitresses cashiers
so many people into whose eyes we never look
  seen only as outlines as we exchange
   polite good mornings indifferent nods
  while they carry on slow tedious work
       sometimes relieved
    by a blaring radio which annoys us

to find your face Alaíde we'll have to look for those
  other
  innumerable faces that we're missing

IV

because we know

that it's not only your face
that's missing from the mirror
the face we'd recognise as yours
or your unknown or long-forgotten face
nor only the face of the chauffeur who was kidnapped with
you
and who must have shared your fate

or fared even worse

at the hands of the soldiers

in Guatemala

there are many   many   missing faces
three   four   eight   ten   twenty every day
who like you   suddenly   vanish   disappear

students   teachers   workers   peasants whose
bodies turn up
riddled with
bullets   tortured   stabbed   strangled
liquidated day by day   with cold efficient rage
and each of these faces disappears from a mirror
is awaited daily   the way we wait for yours
with stubborn   hopeless   hope

(*translated by M. Bogin*)

María Teresa Guarneros *Nicaragua*

I Closed the Door . . .

I closed the door to terror
and the terror remained inside.

Neither Mourning nor Chains

One day
I'll wrap myself up in time
and walk past someone at work
– in the city or countryside –
and not pause to dry her tears
or stay her work.
Perhaps, just then, she won't understand.

Afterwards I'll cloak myself with the rain
and, silently, I'll rain down
all the love I carry within,
and again few will understand.

And I will also
clothe myself with the light
and draw near to a dying child
approaching death
and offer her my hands, my sign,
so when I depart
the child will ask why.

At some time in the future
I will cross this land naked
wounded by its pain and misery,
the cries of poverty.
I'll uphold the banners of light, time and truth
as I go, naked.
With nothing to fear and nothing to hide
– not cold nor hunger nor thirst.
I'll shout as I go
– no, more than just shout,
I'll raise a yell that rises with my blood.

Afterwards
there shall be neither mourning nor chains.
We shall be reborn with another aspect.

That worker, that child
will then understand why.

It's so clear to me:
it cannot be in vain
that we start building
our tomorrow today.

Voices

Voices
voices
thousands of voices
tireless
incessant
follow me obsessively
they accompany
my sleepwalking existence
my discomfort
my icy feet
and my worries
over the comrades
disappeared on demonstrations.

Voices
voices
like needles of rain
silently piercing
forever crying out.

My name begins to appear on lists
they notice me
they call me an accomplice.

We begin to throw dust
to laugh absurdly
to learn new languages
to speak them
without an accent.

We begin to suffer morbid visions
I know deep within
despite your absence and mine
that victory is near.

A free people
a bright country.
Mine is a homeland of memories
yours still of tales told
and a collection of postcards.

We the Children of the Sun

We are the children of the sun are we,
who write in the shadows of evening,
who walk in the dark of the night,
who arise in the light of dawn,
who go barefoot in the womb of the world,
who sow the field,
who grow the daily bread,
who know the language of the wind,
and are learning to fly on a bird's wing.

We are the people whose blood is of lagoons,
whose bodies simmer with volcanoes,
who see the rain fall on a parched land
and on tired faces.

We are those who live the intensity of a look,
who plough the furrows of the old,
who bring the bones to bloom,
who consecrate bread in our own flesh,
who break chains and discover the way.

This Dawn

From over there comes a noise
loud as New Year's fireworks.
But it transpires that it heralds
something altogether more sinister,
> more awaited, unexpected,
> more of a fiesta's bauble
> more grotesque, yet more implicit,
> more nearly unbelievable
> than another incoming New Year.

From over there comes the sound
of something crumbling,
of something starting up,
a sort of pawing
and a last sigh.
> And through the incipient signs of earthquake
> extending its very brightest illumination
> the dawn appeared
> already light,

and everything that had not collapsed
could to the last proudly prove
that it stood erect.

Inscription by the Wayside

Oh pale traveller,
who pause on your journey,
approach now my graveside.
See, then touch the crumbling headstone
of my ecstasy. Be sure to remember
that I sleep here.
And that one glorious day I won through
in love, and that in this lonely twilight
I cannot survive oblivion.

In the New Country

Pain has been our challenge,
and the future our hope.
We build as though composing a poem:
writing, erasing, and creating anew.

Biographical Notes

Claribel Alegría was born in Nicaragua in 1924, but considers herself Salvadorean by parentage and upbringing. She graduated in Philosophy and Letters at George Washington University, where she met her husband and literary collaborator Darwin J. Flakoll. Her publications of poetry, testimony, fiction and essays include the novel *Cenizas de Izalco* (1966), *Aucario* (1955), *Huésped de mi Tiempo* (1961), *Vía única* (1965), *Apprendizaje* (1970), *Pagaré a Cobrar y Otras Poemas* (1973), *Sobrevivo* (1978) and the anthology *Suma y Sigue*. Work available in English includes *Flowers from the Volcano* (translated by Carolyn Forché, University of Pittsburgh Press, 1982), *Poesía Viva* (1984) and *They Won't Take Me Alive* (translated by Amanda Hopkinson, The Women's Press, 1987). *Album Familiar* (*Family Album*), a collection of three autobiographical novellas, is forthcoming from The Women's Press (1989).

Marisela Sánchez Alfonso was born in Havana in 1956. She works as a photojournalist, and has received prizes for both her photography and her journalism in Cuba and Mexico. Her poems have been widely published but her first collection, of love poems, is still forthcoming. She is also working on a photographic book about Yoruba art in Cuba.

Clara Allen was born in Havana in 1926, where she lived until 1950. From 1950–64 she lived in California and thereafter in England. She has worked in higher education and as a counsellor for the Inner London Education Authority. A member of a poetry workshop from 1982–4, her work remains largely unedited.

Rocío América is the pseudonym of Jacinta Escudos, see below. The pseudonym arose while she was working for the revolutionary movement inside El Salvador. The *Poetic Letters* believed found in the pocket of a fallen leader, were originally sent by a sympathiser to the El Salvador Solidarity Campaign, and are addressed to her lover in East Germany with whom she had spent time in exile.

Cira Andrés was born in Camagüey, Cuba in 1954 and qualified at the National School of Art Teachers. Her work has been published in four anthologies between 1982 and 1985. Her first collection, *Visiones*, is forthcoming. She is a member of the Cuban young artists' and writers' organisation.

Diana Avila was born in San José, Costa Rica, in 1952, and studied literature in Peru and drama at the University of Costa Rica. She performed with the *Tierra Negra* and *Cilampa* theatre companies, publishing her poems in magazines and the Ministry of Culture journal. She currently lives and works in New York.

June Beer was a painter and poet from Bluefields on the Nicaraguan Atlantic Coast. Her work first became known after the Sandinista triumph of 1979. She died suddenly in 1984.

Gioconda Belli was born in Nicaragua in 1948, into a bourgeois family who did not learn of her political activism until her escape into exile shortly before the 1979 triumph. Her poetic works include *Sobre la Grama* (1974), *Línea de Fuego* (1978), *Truenos y Arco Iris* (1982) and *De la Costilla de Eva* (1987), and her poems appear in the anthology *Amor Insurrecto* (1984). She has recently completed her first novel, and works with the Association of Nicaraguan Women (AMNLAE) and for the national Nicaraguan broadcasting companies.

Eulalia Bernard was born in Limón, on the eastern seaboard of Costa Rica, of Jamaican forebears. A teacher and one-time cultural attaché in Jamaica, she founded the first Department of Afro-American Studies at the University of Central America, San José. She has also worked in education at the United Nations and as director of television programmes for the Ministry of Public

Education. Her principal publications include *Nuevo Ensayo sobre Existencia y la Libertad Política* (1981) and *Ritmohéroe* (1982). Much of her work is performed, live or on record, with music.

Marilyn Bobes was born in Havana in 1955, and works as a journalist in the cultural department of Prensa Latina, the Latin American news agency. Her published poetic works are *Alguién está Escribiendo su Ternura* (1977) and *La Aguja en el Pajar* (1979). She is active in both the Federation of Cuban Women and in the Saíz Brothers Brigade.

Corina Bruni is Salvadorean. Poems included here are taken from *Altibajos* (Collected Poems 1978–9).

Julia Chavarría is a student and a contributor to the Nicaraguan poetry workshops (see Introduction).

Soledad Cruz was born in Florida, Cuba in 1952. She is cultural correspondent on the daily newspaper *Juventud Rebelde*. Her works include two forthcoming short story collections, *Fábulos por el Amor* and *Jinete en la Memoria* and *Documentos de la Otra* (poetry).

Esmeralda Dávila, a Nicaraguan, is a volunteer soldier in the war against the Contra. Her poetry has mainly appeared in the literary supplements *Ventana* and *Somos*, from which her poems here are taken.

Zaída Dormuz comes from San Carlos, Nicaragua. When she was twelve her first published poem (included here) appeared in the anthology of the *Talleres de Poesía* (Nicaragua 1983).

Maura Echevarría was born in Sensuntepeque in El Salvador. A teacher specialising in the social sciences, she has also worked as a broadcaster and television reporter. Her published poetry includes *Palabras sobre el Fuego, Con el Dedo en la Llaga, Cundeamor, Voces Bajo mi Piel, Sándalo* (1982), and *Ritual del Silencio* (1984).

Jacinta Escudos is the real name of Rocío América, who began writing under her own name after going into exile from her native country of El Salvador. Now in her twenties, she works in an office and writes poetry by night. She is preparing her first poetry collection.

Delfy Góchez Fernández was born in Santa Tecla, El Salvador, in 1958. The daughter of the poet and editor Rafael Góchez Sosa and author and lecturer Gloria María Fernández. In 1977 she entered the Catholic University of Simeón Cañas, San Salvador, to read psychology. Her writing won numerous regional prizes, and in 1976 she won a national poetry competition. She travelled widely in Central America, and became politically dedicated to fighting social injustice. She was killed by the security forces in 1979, during a student uprising and while taking refuge in the Venezuelan Embassy. Her poetry was unedited and unpublished at the time of her death. These poems were given to me by her parents.

Janina Fernández is a lecturer and researcher in the Social Sciences department of the University of Central America. Her writings include *Biografía de una Mujer* (1978) and a poetry collection *Certeza* (1981), which won first prize in the contest Poesía del Certamen Latinoamericano organised by the publisher Editorial Universitaria Centroamericana (EDUCA).

Alaíde Foppa was born in Barcelona of an Argentine father and Guatemalan mother. She travelled widely in Europe and Latin America, settling in Antigua, Guatemala, until forced into political exile in Mexico. She taught Italian literature for many years at the National University of Mexico, co-edited the feminist review FEM, founded the department of Women's Sociology in Mexico, and devised and directed a Women's Forum programme for University Radio. A prominent art and literature critic, she was involved in the international Dante Alighieri Society and in the Institute of Italian Culture. Her poetry collections include *Los Dedos de mi Mano* (1958), *Aunque es de Noche* (1960), *Guirlanda de primavera* (1965), *Elogio de mi Cuerpo* (1970) and *Las Palabras y el Tiempo* (1979). She was disappeared, presumed murdered, by the security forces of President General Lucas on a return visit to Guatemala at Christmas 1980.

Isabel Fraire in a Mexican poet included here because her poem is dedicated to Alaíde Foppa. Born in Mexico City in 1934, she has worked as a literary critic, editor and translator, and has taught philosophy and Latin American literature. Her published works include *Sólo esa Luz* (1969, translated as *Only this Light*), *Seis Poetas de Lengua Inglesa* (1976), *Poemas en el Regazo de la Muerte* (1978, translated as *Poems in the Lap of Death*), and *Pensadores norteamericanos del siglo diecinueve* (1983).

Gloria Gabuardi, Nicaragua, is a poet and militant who works for the Association of Sandinista Cultural Workers. She has one published collection of poems, and is included in the *Poesía Libre* series produced by the Ministry of Culture, and *Las Compatriotas Reparando la Patria* (collected by the Association of Salvadorean Women, published in 1984).

Marta Ivón Galindo is a Salvadorean, at present in exile in the United States where she is a university lecturer. The poems included here are taken from a collection called *The American Dream*.

Ana Ilce Gómez is the only working-class member of the generation of women poets who came of age with the Sandinista revolution. She lives in Masaya with her two children. Her work has appeared in a number of anthologies.

Lilly Guardia was born in Costa Rica. The poems included here are taken from *Sueños de Canela* (1986).

María Teresa Guarneros is a contributor to the Nicaraguan poetry workshops.

Ana Istarú was born in San José, Costa Rica, in 1960. She started writing poetry as a schoolgirl, her first book being published when she was fifteen. Her works include *Palabra Nueva* (1975), *Poemas para un Día Cualquiera* (1977), *Poemas Abiertos y Otros Amaneceres* (1980) and the prizewinning *Estación de Fiebre* (1984).

Claudia Lars is the pen name of Carmen Brannon, daughter of an Irish engineer and a Salvadorean farmer's daughter of Indian origin. Born in 1899, at the age of eighteen she committed her life to writing poetry. Her main publications include *Escuela de Pájaros* (1955), *Fábula da una Verdad* (1959), *Antología Poética* (1962), *Sobre el Angel y el Hombre* (1962), *Del Fino Amanecer* (1967), *Nuestro Pulsante Mundo* (1969), and *Obras Escogidas* (1973).

Carmen Matute was born in Guatemala City. She began writing poetry at forty when she entered the University of San Carlos as a mature student. She joined the publishing group RIN–78, to which most well-known contemporary Guatemalan women poets belong, and with them published *Círculo Vulnerable* (1981) and *Poeta Solo* (1986).

Luz Méndez de la Vega graduated in literature at the University of San Carlos, Guatemala, in 1962, and from the Central University, Madrid, in 1963. She is director of Spanish Literature Studies at the University of San Carlos. She edits the daily Guatemalan cultural supplement, *La Hora*, writes criticism and reviews for other newspapers and magazines, and speaks internationally on art and culture. Poetic works include *Eva Sin Dios* (1979), *Tríptico* (1980), *De las Palabras y la Sombra* (1983), *Las Voces Silenciadas* (1985).

Mezti Suchit Mendoza is the daughter of Salvadorean journalist and writer Rafael Mendoza. At fifteen years of age she is still at school in San Salvador, despite periods of living with her parents in exile. She started writing poetry at the age of twelve; badly physically disabled by a traffic accident, she says she first started writing to express her pain.

Vidaluz Meneses was born in 1944 in Matagalpa, Nicaragua. She graduated in librarianship in the Humanities Department of the Central American University. Her poetic works are *Llama Guardada* (1975) and *El Aire que me Llama* (1982), published when she had taken over the management of the Library and Archives Department at the Nicaraguan Ministry of Culture.

Marienella Corriols Molina is Nicaraguan. Her work has appeared in the literary supplements *Ventana* and *Somos*, from which this poem was taken.

Nancy Morejón, born in Havana in 1944, is a graduate and postgraduate in French and Spanish Literature from Havana University. She specialises in twentieth-century French poetry translation and in the work of her compatriot poet Nicolás Guillén. In 1968 she published her study with Carmen Gonce, of miners in Nícaro, *Lengua de Pájaro*. She has worked for the government and the Union of Writers and Artists (UNEAC). Poetry publications include *Mutismo Amor*, *Ciudad Atribuida* and *Richard Trajó su Flauta y Otros Argumentos*.

Rosario Murillo was born in Nicaragua in 1951, and educated in Britain. Poetry collections are *Un Deber de Cantar* (1981) which won the national Leonel Rugama Poetry Prize and included earlier work drawn from *Gualtayán* and *Sube a Nacer Conmigo*, and *En las Espléndidas Ciudades* (1985). She works as general secretary of the Cultural Association of Sandinista Workers (ASTC) and is co-ordinator of the literary supplement *Ventana*. She is married to Daniel Ortega, President of Nicaragua since 1979, and has eleven children.

Michèle Najlis was born in Granada, Nicaragua in 1946 of Franco-Jewish origins. She graduated from the National Autonomous University of Nicaragua where she now teaches Spanish and Literature. A political activist, she spent periods of exile in Costa Rica until the 1979 Sandinista revolution. Published works include *El Viento Armado* (poetry, 1969), *Augugrios* (poetry and short stories, 1979), and *Ars Combinatoria* (prose, 1987).

Mirna Ojeda is a literacy teacher and contributor to the Nicaraguan poetry workshops.

Cony Pacheco is a nurse, whose work is published through the Nicaraguan Poetry Workshops. She has also been published in *Poesía Libre*, the booklets produced by the Nicaraguan Ministry of Culture.

María Pineda contributed to the Nicaraguan poetry workshops. She is a worker.

Ana María Rodas was born in Guatemala in 1944. She started writing articles at the age of 15, became a journalist, then returned to night school in 1981 and is now assistant lecturer at San Carlos University. She began publishing with the RIN–78 publishing collective in 1983. Poetic works include *Poemas de la Izquierda Erótica* (1973), *Cuatro Esquinas del Juego de una Muñeca* (1975), and *El Fin de los Mitos y los Sueños* (1984).

Reina María Rodríguez was born in Havana in 1952. She graduated in Hispanoamerican Literature from Havana University. In 1973 she joined a writing workshop and in 1975 published *La Gente de mi Barrio*, her first prizewinning poetry collection. *Cuando una Mujer no Duerme* (1980) won further awards. She is an activist in the Communist Youth movement and president of the literary section of her brigade.

Excilia Saldaña was born in Havana in 1946. A graduate of Havana University, she has won numerous literary prizes for her writing for adults and children. Currently working in the publishing house of Gente Nueva and as editor of the magazine *Crónica*, she is also chair of the children's literature department of the National Union of Writers and Artists (UNEAC). Publications include *Cuentos para un Mayito y una Paloma* (children's poetry), *Poesía de Amor y Combate*, *Flor para Amar*, *La Casa de los Sueños*, *La Noche, Mi Nombre* and *El Refranero de la Víbora*.

Christian Santos is a Nicaraguan of the same generation as Belli, Murillo, Najlis and Meneses. A Sandinista militant and activist, her poetry has been widely published, mainly in literary supplements. The poems included here date from her time as cultural organiser to the Río San Juan region in the south-west of Nicaragua. Like many of the other poets, her family was split by the revolution; her husband went abroad, and she has raised her children as a single parent.

Mirta Yañez was born in Havana in 1947. Currently professor of the School of Philosophy at Havana University, she is also a union leader and head of a militia battalion. She graduated in Spanish Language and Literature, and her doctoral thesis on pre-Columbian literature was published by the University of the Andes, Venezuela. She writes poetry, criticism, film scripts, prose and children's stories. Her main publications include *Todos los Negros Tomamos Café* (short stories, 1975), *Las Visitas* (poetry, 1970), and a study of the Latin American romantic novel (1978).

Daisy Zamora was born in Managua in 1950. She graduated from the University of Central America, Nicaragua, in psychology, and studied for two years at the Fine Arts School in León. She has worked as a literature teacher, a gallery director and translator. From 1974 she became active in the *Frente Sandinista de Liberación Nacional* (FSLN), took part in the insurrection of September 1978 and operated *Radio Sandino* for the rebel forces during the final months leading up to the 1979 victory. She has worked during periods of exile on literary reviews in Cuba, Honduras and Mexico, and at home in Nicaragua. Poetic works include *La Violenta Espuma* (1981) and *En Limpio se Escribe la Vida*, (1988). She was Vice-Minister of Culture between 1979 and 1983, and is currently compiling an anthology of a century of Nicaraguan women's poetry.